Modesty and Cunning

Modesty and Cunning

SHAKESPEARE'S USE OF
LITERARY TRADITION

by Karl F. Thompson

Ann Arbor
THE UNIVERSITY OF MICHIGAN PRESS

AD PATREM

Acknowledgments

One of the chief pleasures of authorship follows after the writing, when one reflects on the kindness, aid, consideration, and patience of many friends and colleagues. I therefore happily tender them thanks for encouragement and friendly interest, especially to colleagues at Michigan State University: Dean Edward Carlin, Professors Harry Kimber, Thomas Greer, Harry Hoppe, and George Price. I am greatly indebted to Professor Herbert Weisinger of the State University of New York, Stony Brook, for helpful criticism and advice, and also to Reverend Carl Stratman, C.S.V., of Loyola University. I recall with gratitude mentors whose wise instruction and good counsel resound from times unfortunately too long past: Professors Karl Young, C. F. Tucker Brooke, and Dean William C. DeVane. I acknowledge special indebtedness to Dr. Louis B. Wright of the Folger Shakespeare Library and to the John Simon Guggenheim Memorial Foundation for generous assistance. I have benefited from the skillful and patient assistance tendered me by the staffs of the Folger Shakespeare Library, of the British Museum, and of the libraries of the University of Michigan and Michigan State University. The All-University Research Committee of Michigan State University provided funds for preparing my manuscript. To my wife I offer special thanks for solace and comfort along the way.

KARL F. THOMPSON

East Lansing, Michigan
September, 1970

Contents

. . . an excellent play, well digested in the scenes, set down with as much modesty as cunning.

[HAMLET, II, ii]

I

Introduction

> Suit the action to the word, the word to the action; with
> this special observance, that you o'erstep not the modesty
> of nature: for anything so overdone is from the purpose
> of playing, whose end, both at the first and now, was and
> is, to hold, as 'twere, the mirror up to nature; to show
> virtue her own feature, scorn her own image, and the
> very age and body of the time his form and pressure.
>
> [*Hamlet*, III. ii. 17–23]

"The purpose of playing," Hamlet tells the actors, preparing them for their appearance before the court, is to show "the very age and body of the time his form and pressure." This view of art, which seems at first glance to counsel mere imitation, appears so superficial that we find it difficult to reconcile with Shakespeare's usual practice. We dismiss it as Shakespeare's uttering through Hamlet's words his own professional concern with the problems of directing plays for the Lord Chamberlain's company. Or we further evade the implications of the speech by asserting that Hamlet is talking about histrionics, not dramaturgy. But if all that Hamlet intends to say to the players is "behave naturally," if indeed Hamlet is discussing histrionics only, we must conclude that something is amiss with the characterization of Hamlet. For to have Hamlet say that playwright and actor should concern themselves with recording and employing only those words and mannerisms that men actually use would make him a shallow young man indeed, mouthing the clichés of literary criticism perhaps in vogue among the undergraduates at Wittenberg. Hamlet cannot, even in the mood of the scene, mean only this, and we must take his words more seriously than as a sophomoric truism. For Hamlet is teaching the players and audience alike a lesson often conned but always welcomed by Shakespeare's contemporaries. Hamlet implies a neatly arranged argument: the theater is a mirror of nature; the beholder, perforce seeing himself mirrored in this nature, is at once scrutinizer and a part of the object scrutinized; this scrutiny inspires telltale reactions indicative of the beholder's moral state.

No matter what modern opinion says of the pertinence of this argument to the psychology of theater audiences, we must, for the sake of the play's integrity, believe with Hamlet that plays compel spectators to judge and to react morally. Were this not so, King Claudius's guilty conscience might never have betrayed him, nor would he have had to ask apprehensively about the play Hamlet offers for the instruction and pleasure of the court, "Have you heard the argument? Is there no offence in't?"

The implications of Hamlet's speech for this inquiry into Shakespeare's use of literary tradition spring appropriately enough from the conventional phrase "hold the mirror up to nature." For it is not Hamlet alone who speaks thus of the drama. The same accents sound in innumerable prefaces, apologies, and defenses concerning the stage of Shakespeare's London. To "hold the mirror up to nature" or to record the time's "form and pressure" can mean, to be sure, and too often does mean for us an exercise requiring only the tape recorder and candid camera. But for Hamlet and for Shakespeare and for the Elizabethans generally, the terms meant something other than impartial observation of what happens in the streets, taverns, shops, and homes of the city or on the highways and in the villages of the countryside. The time's "form and pressure" means, rather, the whole age not only in its language and habiliments, but, more importantly, in its beliefs, loyalties, ethical presuppositions through which its spirit gains voice. And, most important meaning of all, through seeing the age as it really is and hearing its voice, the spectator is expected to judge his time. If he judges, he must be impelled to reform, if not the age, at least his own behavior. Thus, the voices of the satirist, the disillusioned commentator, the didacticist sound in Hamlet's speech about the purpose of playing. For to show the age as it truly is will entail revealing not only the morally sound beliefs and customs but the differences between them and the way men actually behave in too often betraying the truths by which they should live. The habit of thus assuming that the audience will judge the nature it sees mirrored is itself a convention, finding expression in the expected didacticism of comedy, tragedy, and romance. And Hamlet's speech moralizes, in the manner characteristic of much of Shakespeare, two meanings in one statement: the time's "form and pressure" means both the loyalty to and betrayal of those beliefs which are, in effect, the soul of the age.

The dramatist can discover the soul of the age, which, so the Elizabethan mind assumed, it is his unavoidable duty to mirror so that it can be judged by his audience, nowhere better than in the books, poems, plays, and stories of his time, without which the deeper attachments to religious, moral, and social values cannot live. These literary forms, the customary forms of expression, must consequently be themselves a vital part of the soul of the age. Hence, any study of the facts and problems concerning Shakespeare must finally take into account Shakespeare as handler of familiar literary conventions, desirous of communicating the lively image of the time. Shakespeare was, to be sure, no different from his fellow dramatists in relying on the familiar expressions of accepted ideas, for the Elizabethan dramatist wrote more often from books than from gardens. Such was his training in school, such was the intellectual temper and habit of the time. Such practice we see, for example, in Euphuism with its oft-repeated comparisons drawn not from observation of nature but from a kind of unnatural natural history found in books and proverbial expressions and moralized catalogs of plants and animals. The characters in plays and books who utter such comparisons are, likewise, types derived from specimens embedded in familiar literary tradition. Shakespeare's audience, moreover, had looked at the same tradition as he. And with dramatist and audience sharing a familiar literary tradition, the soul of the age has a doubly understandable voice and discernible form. Here, then, in the literary tradition is that nature, to mirror which is the purpose of playing.

Shakespeare, as practical man of the theater concerned with the daily manage of his craft, employed this tradition and its attendant conventions with virtuosity and ingenuity resulting in fame and fortune. But he remained committed to the socially and ethically significant ideals metaphorically bodied forth in the conventions. In short, he preserved his world as it existed in the literary tradition; he did not seek overtly to change either the literary tradition or the society of his time. Indeed, his manner of using conventions repeatedly strengthens the tradition, summarizes it, and confirms its social and political, religious and ethical implications. Not a forsaker of the ways that were, but a restorer and invigorator—this is Shakespeare's way with tradition. It might, of course, be said that to strengthen, purify, test, and use conventions more precisely than any other dramatist of his time is to be an innovator of the highest order.

Tradition and convention, slippery terms at best, resist close definition—witness Harry Levin's difficulties in pinning them down in his essay "Notes on Convention."[1] Under the reader's correction, I propose to use them thus: convention I take to mean any detailed familiar character type, turn of phrase, tag line, stock situation, expression, or metaphor; by tradition I mean a body of such conventions that, taken together, make up a coherent, recognizable theme, or type of drama or story, or poetic statement of doctrine, such as the revenge play or courtly romance. I hope to have avoided the extremes, on the one hand, of trying to prove the existence of a tradition by too few examples, and, on the other, of piling up examples so as to overwhelm by sheer weight of citation. For the test of convention, hence tradition, must at last be its ready acceptance resulting from a measure of familiarity.

I make no claim to extraordinary insight or ingenuity in setting out on this investigation of Shakespeare's use of conventional literary materials. We have, after all, sufficient record to show that he borrowed readily and extensively from almost everything he read or heard and that he seized upon certain strands embedded in the web of Renaissance culture and made them more visible to his age, thus revealing in brilliant texture the pattern of the time. We have some excellent guides in trying to judge Shakespeare's success in thus expressing the soul of his age: L. C. Knights's *Some Shakespearean Themes*, Hardin Craig's *The Enchanted Glass*, Harold Goddard's *The Meaning of Shakespeare*, and Donald Stauffer's *Shakespeare's World of Images*. These are all concerned, however, with Shakespeare's plays as statements of themes and mirrorings of the larger perspectives of man's life, whereas I want to focus more directly on Shakespeare's method of incorporating conventional material and traditional patterns into his plays. For Shakespeare ought to be viewed primarily as a man of the theater, extraordinarily busy in the writing and direction of plays. This is not to mock other possible views of Shakespeare, however, all of which have their edifying interest: the Bard of Avon or Shakespeare as lyric poet; Shakespeare, prosperous shareholder in the Globe and burgess of Stratford; Shakespeare, Christian allegorist; plain Will Shakespeare, Englishman; Shakespeare, research scholar and contriver of first-rate plays from inferior sources.

In setting down guidelines for my task, I must first define the sets of conventions of greatest relevancy to Shakespeare's dramaturgy. In doing so, I appeal to the spirit of prudent selectivity. Other treatments of the conventions of the Elizabethan theater have extensively enumerated and copiously illustrated what the Elizabethan reader and spectator would have recognized as the customary form and content of literature: M. C. Bradbrook's *Growth and Structure of Elizabethan Comedy;* Irving Ribner's *The English History Play in the Age of Shakespeare;* Fredson Bowers's *Elizabethan Revenge Tragedy;* Marvin Herrick's *Tragicomedy*. Henri Fluchère in his *Shakespeare* has put us all in his debt for his informed commentary on and exposition of, the whole of the Elizabethan drama's concern with tradition and convention. Rather than rephrase much of this commentary, I want to concentrate on the elements of the literary tradition and its attendant conventions that seem to me most significant. Four such aspects of the tradition promise to afford sufficient sound examples to show how Shakespeare used these familiar conventions and to what effect. The most important of these four sets of conventions on the score of dramaturgy as well as ethical content is courtly romance; second, the conventions that contribute plot and story to the revenge tragedy; third, but perhaps most pervasive of all, the conventionally expressed didactic purpose of the drama; and last, the conventional expressions of the doctrine of natural correspondences, which compose, to use E. M. W. Tillyard's term, the Elizabethan world picture.

These sets of conventions will be defined more fully in succeeding chapters. And, since I claim for Shakespeare's audience a high degree of knowledge of the literary tradition of the time, I try to show that the Globe audience was, as I term it, "a ready audience, well taught." With this kind of audience the dramatist's task becomes at once easier and, paradoxically, more challenging. The dramatist can employ familiar characterizations and themes, knowing that his audience will be agreeably receptive to such statements. But he must try, if he is at all conscientious, to make the audience aware of its agreement that the familiar artistic statement is a sound one by first inducing some kind of debate or division in the consciousness of the auditors that makes their agreement meaningful.

Shakespeare uses conventional material in different ways throughout his career in pretty much the following pattern: first, during his apprentice period before the building of the Globe, conventions appear elaborated and embellished; then come the Globe plays in which the conventions are used in increasingly compressed and abbreviated form; and finally, in the late romances (except for *The Tempest*), the conventions are again employed in an expansive and leisurely fashion. In tracing Shakespeare's use of conventional material, furthermore, I shall compare the methods employed by other dramatists only when a significant point can be made, for an item-by-item comparison and contrast with the plays of Jonson, or Lyly, or Greene, Dekker, Beaumont and Fletcher, and so on,

present such possibilities of multivolume treatment as to stagger
the mind.

I have two consequent matters to deal with from time to
time. One is an investigation of Shakespeare's habit of creating
novel characterizations from conventional types; the second
is a critical examination of the opinion that Shakespeare at
best tolerated conventions and whenever he could so mocked
and maimed them that they expired, an opinion especially ir-
ritating when, as often happens, it is phrased as an offhand
"everyone knows" comment.

Anyone who has read at all extensively in Shakespearean
criticism can recall how overused are phrases extolling Shakespeare's skill in "realizing a character in a dramatic medium,"
or "bringing a character to life." I want to probe behind such
phrases to try to see how Shakespeare actually does create
character, and I want to assess the importance in Shakespeare's dramaturgy of his merging of conventional character
types so as to create a new, vivid (hence more "real") character. In this endeavor the audience's familiarity with conventional characters is of utmost significance. Shakespeare's audience must have come to the theater with a considerable
number of assumptions or preconceptions about the kind of
theme and characterizations it was proper to stage. Since
Shakespeare evidently sent this audience away content with
what they had seen, he must have avoided outraging their pre-
conceived sensibilities. How did he manage this? It is not self-
evident that Shakespeare, having studied the same books that
many in his audience had perused, should have created Arden
and Illyria. But it helps to know that Shakespeare, having employed his schoolboy talents on the same exercises at which
many of the audience had labored, should fashion stories,
themes, and characters from literature not altogether strange
to his audience. It is, actually, self-evident that there was a
more comfortable and assured meeting of minds in the Globe
theater than the modern dramatist can hope for. And it is also
self-evident that turns of speech, sentiments, and motivations
recognizable to the audience will help the character of Hamlet
"come to life" and exhibit a more vigorous "reality of charac-

terization" through assimilating characteristics of disparate
conventional types. The same can be said of the leading characters and the themes of the major plays. Elsinore, Arden,
Illyria—and all such places into which Shakespeare invited
the Globe audience to enter—offered to the view some famil-
iarly reassuring topography and denizens whose countenance,
language, and habiliments were not forbiddingly strange.

In addition to the conventional types Shakespeare incorporates into the characterizations of his plays, however, there
are many conventional themes and statements of belief that
sound to modern ears so unenlightened that we are inclined,
like E. E. Stoll, to dismiss them as merely popular supersti-
tions.[2] Thus Shakespeare is left-handedly complimented for
not really believing what he writes but, for the sake of getting
his audience to listen, giving it from time to time what its unenlightened and often superstitious mind wanted.

Nothing could be more astray from a right reading of
Shakespeare's lines. For all conventions which compose Shakespeare's aesthetic world are sound beliefs. Modern philosophy
and science may prevent our rational acceptance of the notion
of an ordered cosmos and the parallel organization of creation
into macrocosm and microcosm; and modern psychology may
make it difficult for us to fit all of Hamlet's perplexities or
Iago's motives into coherent case studies. But the aesthetic
soundness of conventional beliefs when incorporated into an
artistic form cannot be doubted. That Shakespeare shared the
belief of his age in the matter of macrocosm and microcosm
seems to me self-evident. That he employed such conventions
with aesthetic deliberation in his plays I hope to make evident.
I further hope to show that with modesty and cunning he creates a realm of illusion irresistibly attractive to Elizabethan
and modern audience alike. To create this realm of illusion
and to impart "reality to the illusion" there is needed "reality
of characterization." The reality is the effect made by the character upon the audience at the moment of viewing—and also
in the time of reflection after the play—and not the psychological truth or soundness of the characterization in Freudian,
Rankian, Jungian, or Adlerian terms. And as I have asserted,

the impact of the characterization depends, in Shakespeare's dramaturgy, upon the imagination-stirring blend of familiar conventions.

Nor did Shakespeare ever discard conventions, not even the most tried-and-true love conventions. So annoying is this fidelity to conventions to modern critics, who would like to see Shakespeare grow beyond his patent dependence upon conventions in the early comedies, that they invent a Shakespeare who turns upon the old usages and themes and mockingly does them in. Benedick is seen as a character brought to life by his mockery of the love conventions;[3] even *Two Gentlemen of Verona* is interpreted as an extraction of the last drop of silliness from the love-game comedy; and the romantic comedies are praised for being a therapeutic purge of the audience's unwholesomely adolescent addiction to romanticized fanciful love talk.[4] Here again it is not often seen that Shakespeare, far from abandoning old conventions, becomes increasingly skillful in employing them. Search where we will, in *The Tempest* or in *Love's Labour's Lost*, in *The Winter's Tale* or in *Romeo and Juliet*, the same conventions are evident. It is an illusion that the conventions disappear or are outgrown, an illusion of our own making or of our failure to perceive Shakespeare's cleverness (his modesty and cunning once more at work). Words such as cleverness and cunning, however, seem inappropriate for commending Shakespeare's dramaturgy until it is recalled that a dramatist by the nature of his craft must be an opportunist and must make it his business to be clever in order to govern his audience's responses.

Cleverness, however, does not preclude seriousness of purpose. Such seriousness is universally granted Shakespeare except by those who say that the poet who preaches is an aesthetic monster. Shakespeare does not preach, of course, but often makes his characters do so. How then can any purpose at all be ascribed to the man behind the puppets, who must divest himself of personality in order to manufacture speeches for others, never for himself. If we assume that Shakespeare never believes what he has his characters say, or never shapes their utterances so that a necessary moral as well as aesthetic conclusion is reached in the play, we can say that Shakespeare was not a great thinker or even an original one, was no philosopher in any methodical way, and was careless of ontology and teleology. This view is surely an overreaction inspired by fear of being identified with those who search out and quote the "high truths the Bard has uttered." It makes us nervous to be thought so superficial as to take seriously collections of "noble thoughts in beautiful language."

Shakespeare, however, no matter how little we fancy the terms in connection with poetry, does have a well-developed teleology and ontology. We cannot find them merely by searching out, concordancewise, terms like being, purpose, essence, *terminus ad quem,* or quotations revealing Shakespeare's private beliefs. As has been suggested and will be more fully shown later, the philosophical patterns of the age are expressed in the literary tradition and its conventions. Now if Shakespeare expresses, preserves, and strengthens this tradition, he must necessarily do the same to the moral and ethical content of the tradition and whatever of philosophical import it possesses. Thus to preserve from diminution and waste the ethos of his age surely puts Shakespeare in the ranks of the serious thinkers of his age, certainly far above the rank implied by T. S. Eliot's comment on Shakespeare as a nonphilosopher: "It is not certain that he thought to any purpose."

II

The Gifts of Time:
The Chief Conventions of
Shakespeare's Plays

It would be tidily ordinary to follow the lead of the editors of the First Folio and classify Shakespeare's plays as comedies, histories, and tragedies; then deal with the conventions pertinent to each genre; and, finally, describe Shakespeare's use of the several kinds. Such seemingly neat procedure has lured many a writer into an area of academic quicksand where, struggling to find a firm footing among the shifting discriminations of Renaissance critical theory, the scholar loses sight of the actualities of Shakespeare's stage and the literature available to Shakespeare and his audience. Obsessed with clarifying Renaissance definitions of tragedy, comedy, and tragicomedy, the scholar writes paraphrases of Sidney, Puttenham, Webbe, Wilson, and so on and, to give his learning the right saffron tinge, laces his discourse generously with quotations from Scaliger, Minturno, and Castelvetro. Excellent as such studies are, one wonders if they are not two removes from the day-to-day business at the Globe theater. I propose to try at least to stay within sight of Shakespeare at his writing desk and at the Globe.

If not by categories of dramatic types, how can we best review Shakespeare's use of conventions? The study of source and analogue is tempting, again by reason of its apparent logic, for Shakespeare indubitably hewed close to many a story line and cribbed wholesale characterizations and dialogues. Unfortunately, the notation of conventions as they appear first in the source and then in Shakespeare often leads to mere comparisons of particulars—with inevitable laudatory comments on Shakespeare's changes, which "make a character come to life," and so on. The trouble with this approach is that it must miss as much as it marks. For Shakespeare makes changes in adapting sources under guidance and instruction of the whole tradition and its sets of conventions. He combines, blends, adds subplots, characters, and incidents so as to profit from the audience's familiarity with the conventions, a familiarity (on Shakespeare's part as well as the audience's) bred from acquaintance with similar conventions not only in dramatic but in extradramatic sources—in collections of stories of revenge, for example, and in pamphlets, ballads, even schoolbooks, and sermons. Moreover, there are some aspects of Shakespeare's drama for which the most industrious and ingenious researchers have found no one source. And if Shakespeare creates on his own, without model, source, or analogue, a play (*Love's Labour's Lost*, for example) similar in its use of conventions to a play taken from a well-known source (as *As You Like It* from Lodge's *Rosalynde*), what else can we suppose than that Shakespeare was so used to employing the conventions and so skillful in extracting from them the maximum dramatic value that in filling out any plot he called upon his mastery of the entire tradition and waited not the instruction of particular sources. Thus, in filling out the sketch afforded by a source, in creating the ambience wherein his characters live, where else can Shakespeare be supposed to turn for guidance but to his familiarity with the entire literary tradition. In short, he no more invents the changes from his sources than he invents the plots and characters he borrows outright. His is a wider harvest than study of source and analogue will ever let us see.

Shakespeare (I cannot affirm this too often) exploits and preserves conventions; he neither breaks free of their strictures (a conclusion unfortunately inevitable if we use merely the source and analogue approach), nor fashions novelty in some mysterious way ("the involuntary working of his genius," to borrow a time-honored phrase from Sidney Lee's *Life of Shakespeare*) in despite of contemporary literary critical rules that decreed appropriate decorums for tragedy, comedy, and tragicomedy. In sum, the most practical way to look at Shakespeare's use of literary traditions seems to be to deal first with some of the most coherent sets of the conventions that make up Renaissance literary tradition and then observe Shakespeare's use of these conventions throughout his career.

The most important influence shaping Elizabethan drama during the time that Shakespeare was composing his early plays was the romantic story. The triumph of love over adventure as the chief theme of comedy was completed during the 1590s, and Shakespeare aided this triumph and profited from it.[1] On the surface, the newer comedies were tales of true love, opposition of parents, threats of rivals, lovers' quarrels, the supposed death of one of the lovers, and sometimes the prodigal son theme with love interest added. Stock characters and situations, however, are of less significance than other more durable conventions that give real strength, ethical and aesthetic, to the romance stories whether in prose, verse, or drama. These more durable conventions compose the courtly tradition and lend vigor and fiber to the superficial story line and stock characters of romance.

The origin, growth, and content of the courtly tradition are too well known, however, to need more than brief summation here. There is no need to paraphrase extensively C. S. Lewis's *Allegory of Love*. What is necessary to say is that from its beginning in Provence in the eleventh century and through its dissemination throughout Europe, it developed in its narratives, songs, and poetry conventions which are, in effect, metaphors descriptive of the religious and ethical sanctions of medieval and Renaissance social patterns. There is, first, the feudal metaphor, which terms the lady overlord to her lover, for whom is prescribed the role of vassal owing her fealty and honorable obedience. Ruling over these feudalized arrangements is the lord of love, at whose court recalcitrant lovers are disciplined and reluctant ladies commanded to grant their favor to faithful servants of love. At the court of love the commandments of love are rehearsed so as to teach lovers their duty. Unskillful or tardy lovers are given lessons in deportment and conversation in a school of love. Debates on questions of love and honor are held, and judgments pronounced by the lord of love. The lover must perform praiseworthy deeds so as to be worthy of his lady's favor. Scoffers at love are tried and punished, and their contrition, confession, and penance associate the feudal metaphor with the metaphor of the religion of love (even as in actuality feudalism and religion were interdependent and interpenetrative). Lovers refer to their ladies as saints, objects of veneration. And the creed of this religion is that as love of God is man's eternal good, so *amor* is everything *in saeculo bonum*.

On the continent, especially in Italy, these conventions were enfeebled by the infusion of Platonic notions of love. But fortunately for the drama this did not happen in England to nearly the same extent. The Italianate Platonized verson of love, which with its flight to the ideal is not readily susceptible to dramatization, influenced the Elizabethans' language, to be sure, and *petrarchismo* abounds in their conceits. But dramatic situations, characters, and conflicts remain, in comparison with continental literature, more rather than less medievally romantic and were not Platonized into conversations ending in pale, etherealized renunciations. The Elizabethans evidently preferred the older, hardier conventions in which the conflicts and conclusions of the courtly metaphors were vigorously acted out.

By the time Shakespeare began to write comedy, the native courtly tradition, stemming from Chaucer and elaborated by his fifteenth-century imitators, had replaced the medieval theme of adultery with the romance of marriage, a change happily adaptable to the ethical instructiveness sought for by Elizabethan drama. Not only did romantic comedy edify the intending honest wooer, it promised chastisement for the unworthy and correction for the foolish. Thus the conflict between *amor in saeculo* and sempiternal love was neatly resolved in the bonds of love-in-marriage, and the Elizabethan writer was spared having to compose awkward and unconvincing palinodes.

Another distinctively English change in the courtly tradition was the exploitation, to a degree greater than that dared by continental writers, of the humorous mockery of the love conventions. Clowns, borrowed from the native comedy's Vice and rustic or adapted from the classic comedy's scheming slave, were required to ape their betters and improvise travesties of the code of love. This had, of course, the happy result of disarming adverse criticism, for even if the lowly speak homely truths about the fantasies of lovers, who among the readers or auditors would be of the party of the rude and unlettered? We laugh, but remain safely on the side of the refined, the courtly, the true believers. Seldom has there been a more flexible or more adaptable set of conventions, full of potential conflicts ready to be exploited alike for entertainment, for instruction, and for characterization in tragedy, history, and comedy.

Just as romance came to dominate stage comedy in the 1590s, so did revenge prevail in tragedy. Indeed, there is as much similarity in the provenance of both romance and the revenge story as in the way in which their respective conventions, transferable from genre to genre, are adaptable to traditional purposes of art, that is, to delight and to instruct, as the Elizabethans, under the tutelage of Horace, never tired of asserting. Like romance, the revenge story carries on an age-old theme. Again, the history of the revenge theme is too well known to need more than summary treatment here. No need to retrace and re-expound the findings of so excellent a scholar as, for example, Fredson Bowers, whose *Elizabethan Revenge Tragedy* tells all we need know about the form, its sources, and its variations during Shakespeare's career. We might add L. B. Campbell's *Shakespeare's Tragic Heroes*, and, of course, Muriel Bradbrook's *Themes and Conventions of Elizabethan Tragedy*. From the Greeks the revenge story inherited the central situation of the character in tragedy, more often than not involved in revenge: Achilles' revenge for Patroclus, Orestes' for Agamemnon, Medea's for her wrongs at Jason's hands. With Seneca, more blood and more violence are added, and more of the intrusion of the supernatural becomes evident through the ghost's burdening the living with the duty of revenge. In medieval legend God's vengeance becomes the theme of narratives recounting the punishment of sinners; or Fortune, though sometimes indifferently watching the mighty and proud fall at the turning of her wheel, often finds it gratifying to comment on the dejection of those deservingly encountering disaster, usually with bloody circumstance.

In Renaissance literature revenge is everywhere encountered as the motive of villain and of hero alike. But English dramatists, unlike their French and Italian fellows, took Seneca straight and, save for a small clique of university dramatists, resisted the urgings of commentators on Aristotle to observe a classical decorum by banishing violence and blood from the stage. Even as the dramatists refused to Platonize the conflicts and actions of romantic love, so did they refuse to Aristotelianize tragedy into verbalized dignity. The revenge story, whose characters translated thought and motive into visible and horrendous deed, could, moreover, boast of a classic origin and exemplary decorum of its own in Senecan tragedy. Its continuing efficacy as a medium of narration was testified to by the abundance of stories mirroring the history of great men and their fall, by Italian *novelle* with their motives of love-inspired revenge for the sake of personal honor, and by successful English plays like *Gorboduc* (1562), *The Misfortunes of Arthur* (*ca.* 1587), and *The Spanish Tragedy* (1586).

Revenge tragedy, moreover, like the love comedy, exerted the attraction of an implied direct involvement with problems of individuals in real life. The justification of revenge was a moral issue debated in tracts, in treatises, and in sermons. In this way the revenge story satisfied another important requirement of Elizabethan literature, that is, instruction. Curiously enough, the seriousness with which present-day critics analyze the issues of private revenge versus public justice hints that we can write more easily and dispassionately, therefore with more critical accuracy, about Elizabethan romance than tragedy. For the code that compels a man to seek revenge involves motives that we too can readily understand, whereas romance seems safely distant and we can maintain a more judicious attitude. But in order to discuss revenge tragedy we enlist the aid of the social historian. The result of writing like historians is that our sober analyses depart not a little from literary criticism and become evaluations of the socially unsettling impact of the new politics which saw royal authority usurping the older private responsibility for upholding individual honor and punishing wrongs against one's person. We must take into account, furthermore, such matters as the theologically significant message in the *Book of Homilies* which informed Elizabeth's and James's subjects that God, who watches man's every act, has repeatedly and unequivocally reserved vengeance to Himself and (following the theory of divine right) also to His agents, the monarch, the royal courts, and the crown's officers. No such weighty extraliterary concerns affect our view of romance, which therefore more clearly concentrates upon the art.

If we deal with revenge tragedy in somewhat the same way we did with romance, we can see the tradition embodied in certain conventions which are discussed at length by Bowers and Campbell. From their books we can deduce these important qualities of the Elizabethan revenge play. To provide motive for the action the plot uses the stock characterization of the Machiavellian villain (who gradually comes to dominate the genre and in the plays of Chettle and Marston usurps the chief role that the earlier tragedy of Kyd had assigned to a hero-revenger). A questioning of the ethical rightness of the hero's cause, together with his search for confirmation of his suspicions of foul play, complicates and refines the characterization of the protagonist. Supernatural obligation is imposed on the hero by the visitation of a ghost. And madness, real or feigned, as well as melancholy, often influences the hero's actions and words.

There are also many conventions that afford reassuring familiarity to actor and audience: set scenes of lamentation at the tomb, the wearing of black, premonitions of disaster, ritual swearing, the use of poison, merry executioners turning jests at the block or gallows, repentant murderers who cause quick reversals of the plot, and confidants to whom avengers and villains betray their secret thoughts. These are, however, minor conventions, lending themselves to the history of the revenge tragedy as a catalog of similarities with some variations noted from playwright to playwright.

The most important revenge play convention, for our purposes, because from it the genre draws its essential ethical and aesthetic strength, is the theme of the intervention of the supernatural in men's affairs. As human revenge is the justice sought for in this world, so is divine vengeance the restoring of the gods' intended order. To accomplish this vengeance, the revenger must be obedient to the code of blood revenge, learn his lesson so to speak in the school of revenge, and, often prompted by a ghost's urgings, bring the offender to book. Or, if tainted by the act of bloodletting, the avenger must himself suffer condign punishment even as his victim suffers. The revenger is thus the agent of a higher power, a scourge himself of crime, but a scourge often broken and cast away by the very power that employs it. Throughout tragedy, moreover, runs the theme of the cyclical nature of time and change. Fortune's wheel turns throughout Renaissance as well as medieval literature. This conventional metaphor in a way expresses the traditional belief of a supernatural power guiding the affairs of men, for the goddess Fortune smiles at what she does, and her irresistible force subdues murderer king and triumphant avenger alike.

In discussing the conventions of romance and revenge tragedy, I had necessarily to touch upon the instructive aspect of the tradition, for instruction and moral benefit run like a thread through all Elizabethan discussions of literature. Too often, modern commentators are content to point this out—the didactic purpose is easy enough to illustrate. But it is more to the point to try to show how the Elizabethan writers, especially the dramatists, incorporated didacticism into their work.

In part, the didactic method is an inheritance from medieval allegory and numerous dream visions. However, the nice balance between delight and instruction even then was more often upset than maintained—witness the two sections of even so conventionalized a work as *The Romance of the Rose*, the first part coming close to a balance of delight and instruction, the continuation being by any judgment overburdened with didacticism. It is this kind of allegory (in its decadent form, of course, which seems to mean any dream vision not written by Chaucer) that critics have in mind when in the modern habit they deplore its talkative personifications, its lame humor, its solemn admonitions that virtue is better than vice, and its at best ingenious framework of the vision which puts the reader at one remove from the story. Allegory in its pure form passes, but old habits persist. Elizabethan eyes continue to see that even the most realistically presented characters are in a way personifications of evil and good, of passions and virtues. And every act bears witness, either solemn or witty, to the moral struggle in which men have been commanded by their maker to enlist. We are used to lamenting this habit of moralizing, but we should recall that from the didactic purpose come not only leaden sententiousness but the glories of the *Faerie Queene* and *Arcadia*, those golden worlds, as has been said, by which this world of brass is to be judged.

The conventions which transmit this didactic aspect of the literary tradition are, most notably, the characterizations originating from epigrammatic lines and speeches, or commentary enunciated by characters as they observe some event or respond to speeches of another character. These comments in turn derive from the Elizabethan writer's assurance that the reader and listener would expect to be edified, hence improved by the example set before him. There is, perhaps, no better way to summarize this part of the tradition than by quotation of several writers whose words indicate the permeation of all forms of literature by the instinct for didacticism. First, as is suitably deferential to his learning and high station, is Sir Philip Sidney. I cite not his well-known definition of tragedy but his comment, in his *Defence of Poesie* (1583), on comedy as "an imitation of the common errors of our life which he [the comic poet] representeth in the most ridiculous and scornful sort that may be, so as it is impossible that any beholder can be content to be such a one."

Thomas Heywood in his *Apology for Actors* (1612) ascribes a similar morally corrective function to tragedy, which will "terrifie men from the abhorred practice" of "notorious murder." In like terms speak Webbe, *Discourse of English Poetrie* (1586); Puttenham, *Arte of English Poesie* (1589); Sir John Harington, *Apologie of Poetrie* (1591). And so say the dramatists Chapman and Massinger, to name just a couple. So also says Hamlet, implicitly, to the players. Sir Walter Raleigh in the Preface of his *History of the World* (1614), speaks for all contemporary chroniclers: "Wee may gather out of History a policy no lesse wise than eternall; by the comparison and application of other mens forepassed miseries with our owne like errours and ill deservings." For popular writers John Taylor's verses commendatory to Heywood's *Apology for Actors* will suffice:

> *A Play's a brief Epitome of time*
> *Wherein man may see his virtue or his crime*
> *Layd open, either to their vices shame,*
> *Or to their virtues memorable fame.*
> *A Play's a true transparent Christall mirror,*
> *To shew good minds their truth, the bad their terror.*

Prince Hamlet would applaud the thought, if not the meter, especially so since he hoped to show the king's bad mind its terror.

A handy convention for translating instructive doctrine into dramatic statement is the stock character. The social types of classic comedy, the braggart for example, are especially useful in this connection, for they serve as butts of the instructive commentary of the wiser sort. Similarly in romantic comedy, the inept or foolish lover is laughed out of court, the jests of the wiser in love's lore affording the audience warning about how not to behave. Some stock characters are straightforward examples seriously intended: the good ruler in chronicle accounts and the honest lover of romances. These, however, are less obviously effective as monitory examples than the comic types, who are more efficacious teachers because they add delight to instruction. In addition to the serious didacticism effected by the exhibition of reprehensible examples of viciousness and folly, and, in lighter vein, by jests at the expense of fools and knaves, there is, especially in history and revenge plays, an iteration of epigrams and bits of received doctrine. For in history plays there must be some approbatory statement of the dependence of the commonwealth on the respect for kingship, and in the revenge play must occur some acknowledgment, direct or implied, of the royal and divine prohibition of private revenge.

Such variety marks the dramatists' practice that we are likely to miss the importance in their work of this tradition of didacticism. Haphazard in their method of play construction some of them undoubtedly were, but even the most aimless of them thought he was observing dramatic decorum by using in any play regardless of whether it was comedy or tragedy all of these conventions so as to improve the moral health of the audience, which was, of course, the Renaissance notion of the goal of literature. The most effective teaching combines instruction by precept with instruction by exhibition of examples. The most impressive examples are those that unite delight with instruction. And it is more important to add the delight afforded by the comic types to history and tragedy than it is to observe a different decorum for each type of drama. Thus the dramatists, under the weightier demands of teaching, felt it not only allowable but necessary to mix comedy with tragedy and history and romance.

Such practice, however, still puzzles modern writers, who nevertheless acknowledge its effectiveness. How, it is wondered, can we account for the Elizabethan dramatists' mixing of genres in violation of critical admonition to observe the decorum of literary types unless they did so at first intuitively and kept on doing so because their earlier ventures succeeded. A better answer is that it was not the opportunism of these writers for the popular stage but the license given by the weighty Horatian admonition that encouraged such practice. Audience and playwright were consciously satisfied that delight and instruction could and should be combined. Greene summed it up very well when he overwhelmed the authorities cited by scholarly critics of the drama by boldly using as his motto the Horatian *Omne tulit punctum qui miscuit utile dulci.* What Horace meant, of course, was that the delight had to be appropriate, pertinent, and part of the structure of the poem or play, requirements that proved too much for Greene's talents, as indeed they did for all writers of the second order, who lacked the ability to meet the expectations of the active moralists who constituted the Globe theater audience and knew that drama, whether history, comedy, or tragedy, should contain entertainment properly conjoint with instructive conclusions.

An even more important question, however, than why the dramatists persisted in mixing tragic and comic is what were they trying to say in their passages of instruction? What moral was to be illustrated or truth upheld, what verity mocked and twisted by villains to base ends and redeemed at last by the actions of the just? For all the methods of plotting, the evocation of character by discussion, debate, and conflict, the patterns of imagery, the acting out of the metaphors of the religion of love and the code of revenge, all must have some direction and purpose, some agreed-upon tradition, ethical and religious, if the dramatist is to propose and the audience to accept dramas worth looking at. Some principle understood beforehand must be available, not needing lengthy explication in every play but brought to the theater by both playwright and audience and succinctly communicable by conventional phrases and metaphors. This scheme of things-agreed-upon we can find described in E. M. W. Tillyard's *Elizabethan World Picture.* Abbreviated and oversimplified his book may be (it has been so criticized), but there are few better insights into the Elizabethans' conception of themselves and their environment. Some, like A. C. Bradley, have used the term "world order" to describe this background against which

Shakespeare's heroes and villains posture and declaim. Others, like E. E. Stoll, have objected to the assumption that in Shakespeare we see depicted a generally accepted notion of an external and internal harmony of man and nature. For coincidence, often carelessly employed by Shakespeare to eke out deficiencies in plot and sketchy characterizations, has been taken as evidence of a belief in a world order. This, Stoll asserts, is to distort the Elizabethan image of the world for our own philosophical and critical purposes.[2]

Stoll, nevertheless, has to admit that characterization is indeed generated from references to external nature.[3] In Macbeth's "expressions borrowed from his environment," for example, we see the "traditional external nature of the conscience" congenial to the Elizabethan way of thinking but invisible to modern psychologists, who on the basis of the imagery of Macbeth's speeches take him to be a coward, hypocrite, sentimentalist, or whatever they choose. Nor can Stoll deny (though he tries to minimize) the powerful effect of this habitual reference to external nature when crucial matters of plot and character are in hand. Acknowledging the existence of "a superstitious notion not then extinct" that the fall of kings and like disasters to the state were portended or accompanied by upheavals in nature, either in sympathy or revulsion, he suggests that for Shakespeare this was merely a means of emotional emphasis.[4] But he then goes on to say, again citing Macbeth as example, that such upheavals awaken echoes within characters. The point is that not even a hardy skeptic like Stoll can altogether ignore the significance of the Elizabethan belief, moral as well as poetic, in a world order related to men's affairs, an order whose impairment forebodes chaos again threatening in the universe. This belief is an essential ingredient in the writings of the cosmographer, in the imagery of the sonneteer, in the historical examples advanced by the writer on statecraft, and, indeed, in the writing of the theologians. The reforming Calvin himself in his *Institutes* (I. 14. par. 20, for example) compares in conventional terms God's heaven and earth with an orderly and well-furnished house given to man as a goodly habitation.

Tillyard's book is especially rich in citation of such comparisons. I find, moreover, no better term than Tillyard's "doctrine of correspondences" to refer to the basic and most useful metaphors for this world view in which the microcosm man corresponds in little to the macrocosm. Everything within this frame of being can serve as a basis for edifying. Take, for example, one with which all writers were acquainted: the garden of the world and man the gardener. The unweeded garden is, metaphorically, the world of man's lapsarian state. Other comparisons naturally follow. All animals have their correspondence to emotions or sentiments. All animals have their characteristic qualities, and all are correspondent to some aspect of man's moral and emotional being. The movement of planets, the raging of storms and tempests are all correspondent to man's changing fortunes and, furthermore, echo or presage acts of political significance, the order of the heavens being correspondent to the order of monarchy and civil peace.

This kind of imagery fills the speeches of many characters, especially in the histories and the tragedies. For us of the scientific age, who have discovered the law of probability but lack the wisdom or wish to make any coherent correspondence of nature and ethics, this doctrine of correspondence is a matter of footnotes and explication. It takes a book like Tillyard's to afford insight into what the doctrine really meant for the Elizabethan reader, schoolboy or adult, or member of the Globe audience. We can comprehend to a certain degree, at least, what intense delight they took in the entrancing variety yet deeply reassuring orderliness of the correspondences between man and the domain of nature.

Expressions of this doctrine become conventional, of course, and looked for as the worthy utterances of kings and courtiers in chronicles and history plays. Villains, moreover, are at once identifiable by their jeering at the natural portents of disaster that other men heed. Disbelief in and mockery of the proper correspondence of microcosm and macrocosm are evident in the words and deeds of the Machiavellian hypocrite and his forebear the Vice. Their threats of engineering disorder and the efforts of good rulers to restore order and proper correspondence of the body politic and harmony of nature furnish a series of conflicts with which to shape a narrative or a play. And so it goes, pervading, even as the didactic purpose does, all of Elizabethan literature. Shakespeare will use the doctrine of the correspondences to deepen the tone of his tragedy and history even as he will use the metaphor of the religion of love to impart dignity and strength to his comedies. Indeed, the two aspects of the tradition are much alike: for as the religion of love metaphor refers to an ideal orderliness and decency in men's private lives, so does the metaphor of natural correspondence indicate an ideal orderliness and decorum in their public and political lives.

Much has had to be omitted from this summary of what I take to be the most important aspects of the literary tradition as far as Shakespeare's dramaturgy is concerned. But I have, I trust, set out in some degree of coherence these four sets of conventions and their interrelatedness: the courtly tradition and its code of conduct to give characterization and motive and plot to comedy; the revenge story to do the same for tragedy; the tradition of didacticism to give the impulse for audience and dramatist to meet in the theater; and, to give the content of the didacticism, the traditional expressions of or teachings about the orderliness of God's plan seen in nature and, potentially, in man. Finally, we must recall that these conventions can be, and are, used wherever and whenever the dramatist's experience tells him they are appropriate, regardless of critical precept or restriction of scholarly authority concerning the different literary genres.

III

A Ready Audience, Well Taught

The people who thronged into Maiden Lane to tender their pence at the Globe had come from all over London, crossing the river by the bridge or by the fleet of skiffs and wherries, or converging through the lanes and paths of Southwark. A mixed lot, to be sure, consisting of the literate and semiliterate and probably made up of the same faces that had appeared at the door for last week's play and the play before that. That this audience was, on the whole, the same for most plays at the Globe is of equal importance with its being recruited from almost all of the levels of Elizabethan society. For the patrons of the Globe habitually brought with them much besides a mere desire to be entertained and to idle away a few hours. They also had a lively memory of themes and conventions, stock characters and situations, and accustomed metaphors in the many plays they had seen. Hence, they arrived with some expectation that the playwright and actors would be as adroit in handling those themes and conventions as the writers of prose and verse. They would not, therefore, be eager always to applaud works of mere pastime.

It seems fair to test any audience, modern or Elizabethan, by the kind of play it commends. The applause that resounded in the wooden O can be heard, somewhat muffled by time to be sure, but nevertheless vigorous, in such statistics as can be deduced, for example, from Henslowe's accounts of daily receipts, which indicate that Shakespeare's company undoubtedly prospered better than any with whom Henslowe had dealings, and from the very dimensions of the Globe that sug-

gest the shareholders' expectations of profit.[1] All of these indicate the popularity of many of the same plays that have survived in critical esteem to this day. The London audience,
both groundling and gallery, responded, apparently, to the
most difficult and complex poetic statements and was stimulated evidently more often above its usual capacities by Shakespeare at the Globe than by Munday and Dekker at the Rose.
That sensitive hearts could at times dwell beneath rough or
modest exteriors as well as beneath the noble's cloak or
scholar's gown puzzled many contemporary dramatists made
self-consciously uncertain by the scornful comments of littera-
teurs who jeered at mere writers for the playhouses. Contemporary observers and commentators, Gosson and Stubbes and
the like (and modern critics as well), overlooked the stimulating influence of the ingenious use of familiar conventions
upon the audience's sensibilities. Long acquaintance with literary conventions, which were essentially the same in ballads,
romances, and plays, must have generated, even among those
lacking formal education, some capacity to appreciate a dramatist's deft use of those conventions. Hence, the Globe spectators, when they saw *Hamlet*, were not gazing at something altogether new and therefore above the comprehension of all
save the most intellectually nimble. For the generality at the
Globe came not as strangers but as more or less expert appre-
ciators of literary and dramatic skill. The grocer from the City,
his lady and his lady's maid, and the apprentice, as well as the
sophisticate from the Inns of Court were, none of them, so hapless that mere novelty could impress them, as it seemed often
to impress the educated foreign visitors who, unused to a public theater, wondered in their letters and diaries about the mar-
vels of the London stage.

The very fact that Shakespeare was the most successful
dramatist of his time suggests that audiences could not have
been, as has been sometimes assumed, hopelessly divided between the gentles and the clowns, between the true Shakespeareans and the rude pit folk who laughed at the wrong
places and applauded for the wrong reasons.[2] That this division did not exist is further indicated by the remarkably uni-

form literary experience of the Elizabethans, especially as far as the conventional and traditional bases of that literature are concerned. Not that they all necessarily perused the same book, heard the same sermon, read the same poetry, had seen the same play (though all of these are true to a degree beyond the experience of modern times). But they had all read the same kind of story, seen the same type of play, and encountered familiar doctrine in sermons. One need not assume, therefore, as some present-day scholars have been tempted to do, that any one book furnished audience and playwright their ideas on any particular subject. Their common preoccupation with the code of revenge and their belief in the dangerous sinfulness of private revenge do not stem solely from the doctrines expounded in, for example, the dedication and preface of Thomas Beard's *Theatre of God's Judgments* (1597). For the code, and its repudiation, had been assimilated into culture in such a way as to furnish Beard his ideas and the dramatist and audience theirs. By the time a treatise is written, in short, the theater audience has already been pretty well instructed by its own experience with many stories, sermons, ballads, and so on, to the point where it can easily recognize standard, conventional expressions of received opinions.

Prejudgments of the Globe audience have, moreover, biased many analyses of Shakespeare's plays. *Hamlet*, it is said, must have been philosophy and poetry to the judicious spectator; to the groundling, melodrama. The result of this approach must be to misunderstand the structure of the play, hence lose a great part of the meaning of the play itself. For if part is a conscious appeal to intelligence and refined emotions susceptible to poetic imagery, and part condescends to popular liking for blood, action, and noise, Shakespeare stands condemned as an aesthetic hypocrite, a charge which seems not to have been intended by denigrators of the Elizabethan audience. Actually there was no more a dichotomy in the audience than in the play. Melodrama (and the tests of skill and endurance in the bear garden) appealed alike to courtier and commoner. If a bourgeois Ben Jonson was a rarity of his class, so also was the noble Sidney of his. We know pretty well

that there was a unity of taste, a general capacity in the audience at the Globe that was shared by the court too.[3] Hence,
instead of patronizing the city commoners by saying that many
of them could understand a Shakespearean play, we ought to
condescend to the overdressed, arrogant ruffians at Whitehall
and Hampton Court and say that despite appearances they
had intelligence and sensitivity enough to appreciate *Macbeth*
to somewhat the same degree as the demanding, experienced,
knowledgeable Globe audience composed mostly of shrewd
commoners.

But surely, says the believer in unappreciated genius who
relishes what is caviar to the general, surely these are large
claims, wholly beyond the realm of hard proof. Perhaps so, but
no more removed from hard proof than the opposite supposition that Shakespeare succeeded in spite of the majority of the
audience. Nevertheless, such large claims for the audience require some substantiation. Fortunately, we do have considerable indication that the Globe audience was pretty much a
cultural unity. First, we have a record of what kind of education a large part of this audience was likely to have had.
Second, we can infer its preferences fairly accurately because
we can discover the literary tradition which served the Elizabethan age as the reflection and projection of its moral and
emotional being. Shakespeare was a beneficiary of that tradition as well as contributor to it. Moreover, he neither rebels
against nor scorns this tradition or the audience with which
the conventions of this tradition permit him to communicate.
He thinks in remarkably close terms with the judicious spectator, whose schooling has been given edge by schoolmasterish
minds like Colet or Erasmus, whose morality has been enlarged by lessons from the English Bible, and whose imagination has been stirred by romances of knightly adventure; who
has, moreover, tested many plays before—this is your judicious
spectator, and he is a formidable person for the playwright to
encounter, especially so since there were so many of him at the
Globe. To him is owed the success attendant upon the long
struggle of the drama to establish itself as an independent art
and not an appendage of court or noble patronage.

Perhaps the most impressive evidence, however, that the patrons of the Globe composed this ready audience, well taught, is the extraordinary spread of learning in the latter part of the sixteenth century, one of the first fruits of the Renaissance (and Reformation too, which put Scripture in English into the hands of common people). The Globe audience was of London, with recruits from the country by way of the Inns of Court or apprenticeship in the city guilds. In London, literacy must have grown remarkably. What else can be deduced, for instance, from such evidence as the large number of stationers, ninety-seven in 1557 privileged by the Company of Stationers to print and sell books. If we conservatively estimate the population of London during the second half of the sixteenth century at 150,000 to 200,000, there must have been one bookseller for about every two thousand citizens—either a tremendous oversupply or a very impressive demand. It was probably the latter, if we may judge from the Stationers' regulations which permitted an annual printing of 10,000 copies of schoolbooks like Lily's *Grammar*, with allowance for supplementary impressions as needed.[4] This growth of the printing trade accompanies an increase in schools, which trained youths thronging to employment in church, state, and perhaps most important of all for the success of the popular theater, in trade, where employers increasingly demanded that apprentices have what would be roughly equivalent to present-day secondary school education.

It is all very well, however, to cite popular demand for primers and easy books, but what about the heavy books, those demanding diligent perusal as well as high price from their readers? Do they not appear more often in references of modern literary historians than on the shelves of Elizabethan homes? Actually, the demand for one of the most expensive books of the time, John Speed's *Theatre of the Empire of Greate Britaine* (1611), was sufficient to see it through five printings of its *Historie of Greate Britaine* and three of the *Theatre* proper. Works such as Holinshed's *Chronicles* and Hakluyt's *Voyages* and Stow's *Survey of London* all ran through many editions.[5]

Those who thronged to the Globe of an afternoon, drawn by the reputation of Shakespeare's company, expected a measure of excellence in a play that would delight and instruct. They were, for the most part, beneficiaries of an educational tradition that by the 1580's was pretty well established and from which Shakespeare himself had profited. Schoolmasters everywhere throughout England pressed the same kind of book on their students. The schoolmasters and the writers of the texts vied in their efforts to state ingeniously the moral purpose of education, and everywhere grammar schools taught the same subjects with the same intention. That intention swayed the minds even as it certainly guided the pens of all writers on education during the sixteenth century. The spirit of Erasmus, schoolmaster to the Renaissance, hovered everywhere, prompting the writers of texts to fashion books embodying as models the lives of good men, but also citing lives of the wicked and notorious as containing profitable examples of moral errors, hopefully to be avoided. But most striking of all, and of major significance for the training of the writers, readers, and audiences of the sixteenth century, was Erasmus's practice, followed by many other composers of exemplary texts, of citing dialogues and letters as ways of increasing the students' skill with language. Let the pupil suppose himself to be in the same situation as the person of the monitory example, confronted with a dilemma of social and ethical importance; then let him compose a suitable conversation or pen a letter that will explain the moral issues involved and propose an acceptable solution.

If one were to seek for a compendium of literary conventions, of stock situations and characters, of ready-made and formulated opinions, he could hardly do better than to peruse Erasmus's *De Conscribendis*. In it he will find, among many other helps to social and mental improvement, what is in effect a digest of themes and conventions of the code of love as the Renaissance elaborated it. Lads of school age were encouraged by Erasmus to compose letters to their imagined loves, exhibiting alike the profundity of their emotion and of their despair, filling their lines with praise of famous and chaste

ladies who yielded at last to love's importunities, and begging
their loves to look with kindness on them.[6] With a few exercises of this sort, a lad of parts would be well equipped to
mouth the conventions of wooing, to listen appreciatively to
stage lovers' phrasings of the old pleas, or, perhaps, if he were
a lad of merry disposition and superlative talent, to write
either romantic comedies or satirical lines upon the conventions of romance, according to his whim or the mood of his
audience and the demands of the story.

The same sort of teaching by precept, example, and imitation went on throughout the boy's years in school. Stock situations, stock characterizations, themes, phrases, sentiments re-
peat themselves in his schoolbooks. A fund of more or less
moralized contemporary stories, moreover, was added to the
stories of antiquity and mythology. Among these occurred
some alarming examples, a tribute perhaps to the liberal mind
of the schoolmasters of the time. Who nowadays would think
of admitting into required reading for a high school course a
story as lurid as the tragedy *Titus and Gisyppus,* a tale drawn
from Boccaccio of a youth who on his wedding night and out
of amiable regard for his friend's desperate lovesickness yields
his bed and bride to his friend. Thomas Elyot included the
story in his *Governour,* a treatise on education, as conducing
to a proper attitude toward the moral beauty of true amity.
Nor would many present-day educators praise the moral value
of the dramas on which Richard Mulcaster's boys at the Merchant Taylors school spent so much time. So adept were these
boy players that, like the boy companies later at the Black-
friars Theatre, they appeared on terms of equality with profes-
sionals. Six times at least, Mulcaster sent his boys, in response
to command, to play at court. The play chosen for 1583, for
example, was an Italianate romance, *Ariodante and Geneuora,*
a bit beyond the usual schoolboy Plautus.[7] This was probably
the story which Shakespeare used for the Hero and Claudio
intrigue of *Much Ado about Nothing.* To modern minds it
smacks rather more of entertainment than moral instruction.
Whatever the judgment, however, on its literary and ethical
merits, the play must have afforded an excellent example of
use of romantic conventions.

What besides instructive stories of crime and punishment and the exercise of the pen in set dialogues and character sketches (in effect, the composition of rudimentary dramatic scenes) did the boy learn who had progressed beyond his *ABC* and *Primer?* For the most part, a standard course in selected Latin classics, including a considerable amount of drama: in the lower grammar schools, passages from Terence, a great deal of Plautus, and the more modern, for Shakespeare's time, Mantuan; in the upper grammar schools, Ovid, Vergil, Horace, Juvenal, Seneca (drama again), Martial, and Persius. Here is the "small Latine" with which Shakespeare was endowed, and which, according to L. C. Knights, the majority of the Globe audience may well have been able to recollect.[8] The spectators' minds must have been filled with the tags and references to mythology, Senecan depictions of Hades and its errant ghosts, and Ovidian accounts of the gods and the goddesses. These classical references nowadays, as a result of the unhappy history of western culture, are occasions for footnotes in editions of Shakespeare, whereas in actuality they were not very esoteric. Shakespeare, moreover, employed only the more easily recognized and avoided the merely recondite lest they be lost on an ear keeping pace with changes of scene, action, motivation, and characterization.

It seems strange to modern minds, bemused by professional educators' assertions that practical education means the application of talents to the world of things, that tradesmen should have so enthusiastically accepted the pedagogues' grammar school and university prejudices when they granted their support to the guild schools and to new foundations. They nevertheless insisted on a course of studies which included the same "small Latine and lesse Greeke" taught at Shakespeare's Stratford grammar school. The Merchant Taylors School with Richard Mulcaster as its headmaster proposed in its statutes, 1561, to engage in the "bringing up of children in good manners and literature," as if deportment and letters were interdependent. And the Mercers Company had earlier, at the urging of Colet, lent its auspices and supervision to St. Paul's School.[9] Perhaps it was mere prudence on the part of the guild masters and not some article of the creed of humanism that led them to underwrite such ventures which exposed youths to lessons of virtue in schoolbooks and hopefully inspired in these youths like inclinations. At any rate, a not inconsiderable number of these youths must later have applauded the poetic justice they saw daily acted out at the Globe. Indeed, the support of grammar schools and poor scholars at these and at the universities became a pious obligation for well-to-do merchants. The many philanthropists praised by John Stow in his *Survey of London* (1598) were businessmen convinced that godliness and virtue, and a knowledge of letters and Scripture, were matters of practical concern. Literature guided the charity pupil at a grammar school to virtue just as surely as it did the young man at the Inns of Court. It was, indeed, a notion in which the whole of Elizabethan society invested belief, time, and money—considerable of that investment to the mutual profit of the Globe audiences and Globe shareholders.

The flood of books from the presses and shops around Paul's Churchyard, the generally recognized importance of education, the comparatively high level of literacy (probably higher than in the eighteenth century), and more specifically, complaints of conservative educators that common schools were receiving poor boys, thus deflecting the lads from their more proper menial employment, all constitute fairly convincing evidence that city folk, including many of the servant class, were literate. If they read, they must certainly have been indoctrinated with the belief that they were being morally benefited. For the assertion that literature by its precept and example was a lesson in virtue occurs everywhere, from Sidney's elegant phrasings to the tag lines of the most naïve balladeer. The assertion became, indeed, a convention in itself, and many an address to the gentle reader assured him that the violence and depravity and error he was about to peruse would tone up his moral fiber. The gentle reader or judicious spectator, his mind reassuringly soothed by this familiar address, was undoubtedly often unaware of its full implications— save when Shakespeare, for example, has Hamlet strenuously assert the moral relevance of art to life and insist on proving his point by entrapping the king's conscience or by musing on a bookish argument about being or not-being.

Of at least equal significance with this evidence of widespread literacy is the content of what was read. We look at a hypothetical list of best sellers for the 1590's and early 1600's and find—to the chagrin of the decriers of the popular taste of our commoner-ancestors—that it compares quite favorably with a list of books most widely read by the middlebrows of our own decade. It consists of nonfiction and plays as well as fiction, and the major difference is the greater number of religious books and tracts of straightforward moral admonition.

The most practical way for a man to use his skill in reading was, to the Elizabethan way of thinking, to study a book, pamphlet, or story justifying the ways of God to man. An inheritance from the Middle Ages and refurbished with Renaissance topicality, the theme of God's hand being always present in the traffic of everyday life comfortably assured all readers that the Deity was attentive to every act for good or ill performed in the theater of the world. Where else, then, could one find more inspiring literature (or more interestingly sensational anecdotes for that matter) than in the numerous accounts of God's judgments meted out daily, in the past and in the present, to deserving sinners for the obvious edification of the righteous or the would-be righteous. This is the burden, for example, of Thomas Beard's *The Theatre of God's Judgments . . . Augmented by more than three hundred Examples* (1597). Among these three hundred exemplary judgments is an account, edifying but false, of Christopher Marlowe's death. True, a reader of this book might contract some antitheater prejudice from the association of the atheist Marlowe and stage players, but he would at least be aware that the theater was a considerable force in his political and ethical environment.

The common reader thus assured of ethical guidance knew that under the compulsion of social codes men had long acted in violation of God's clear commandments. The public conscience, seeking instruction, discovered, for example, what God's will was in that most agitated problem of the discrep-

ancy between a code of private honor and public submission
to the authority of pulpit and crown. Refer all things to God
had been a satisfactory guide for the medieval mind and continued to satisfy the Elizabethan and Jacobean conscience.
Thus, the common reader of the time, heir to a literary tradition abounding in stories of murder and revenge, understood
that revenge was God's prerogative, whose judgment, he knew,
needed endless repetition to pierce the dull ear of others, if not
his own. One of the best examples, embodying the gist of earlier arguments and being therefore a summary of the genre,
was John Reynolds's *The Triumph of Gods Revenge Against
the Crying, and Execrable Sinne of Murther* (1621–23). Man's
unaided moral sense cannot distinguish between revenge and
murder, says Reynolds, but with God's intervening judgment
and action, revenge and justice can be harmonized. No play-
goer at the London theaters was indifferent to this problem,
and none would deem morally sound any play about revenge
that did not in some way reinforce the same beliefs that
Reynolds urged.

The literature of the Renaissance was, in a manner of
speaking, remarkably old-fashioned, harking back either to the
classics or to medieval conventions. The Middle Ages stubbornly resisted extinction, especially in popular literature, and
evidently neither the judicious spectator at the Globe nor the
general public was averse to perusing tried-and-true themes
embodied in antiquated forms. The simplest theme imaginable
was the promise of God's judgment against sinners; the simplest form, the old-fashioned allegory. Add to the venerable
personifications of medieval literature a few up-to-date embodi-
ments of sin and you will have added novelty, therefore delight, to the familiar instruction. Such was the attempt of
Richard Bernard, whose book, although late for our period,
has such an engagingly typical and explicit title one cannot
help quoting it: *The Isle of Man; or, the Legall Proceedings
in Manshire against Sinne* (1626). In this, medieval types like
Idolatry and the Seven Deadly Sins assault Virtue. But they
are not alone in their attack, for more modern wrongdoers,
Machiavelli and a Sir Plausible Civil, rally to the cause of evil.

But Sheriff True Religion brings the malefactors before the bar to be judged by Lord Chief Justice Jesus.

Such books were a bit removed, by reason of their form— either prosaically didactic or allegorical—from immediate contact with the streets, lanes, homes, and shops of London. As if to take advantage of an opportunity for scoring an immediate and powerful impression, the pamphleteers urged the readers to consider the lessons of religion embodied in personal confessions. This was no idle reading, but full of practical benefit in two ways: it reassured, because God will certainly forgive the pentitent; and it informed about the nature and variety of sin with lively examples drawn from the contemporary world. God kept His eye on sinners, especially on pamphleteers like Robert Greene, who informed the patrons of the bookstalls around Paul's Churchyard of his brushes with temptation, his almost annual yielding, and his timely changes of heart. The year 1590 was especially trying for him, what with *Greenes Mourning Garment* and *Never too Late*. In 1591, however, he bids *Farewell to Folly*. In 1592 he counsels against sin and, incidentally, pays off a few private scores with *A Groatsworth of Witte Bought with a Million of Repentance*. Then apparently, though the authorship is disputed, he writes, as if making sure he has been heard once more before he dies, *The Repentance of Robert Greene*.

Regarding these pamphlets as primarily, rather than incidentally, personal utterances (for we see such things darkly through the glass of modern conventions), we fail to appreciate them as survivals of the medieval confession. We should, moreover, mistrust confessions, however personal they seem, made by a writer whose plays are populated throughout with stock characters. Stock confessions will fall as easily from his pen as stock romantic figures and situations. Indeed, Greene exploited such devices at every turn. The traditional confession, for instance, gave him a conventional and useful form; it also gave the reader a serviceable moral application, if not to himself, yet to another erring mortal. It provided, moreover, a welcome bit of topical gossip and scandal. A convention that has this threefold appeal will not be abandoned by a shrewd writer, especially by one whose artistic conscience is pliable. Such a writer does not really respect his reader and will at best exploit conventions unimaginatively, leaving them pretty much as he finds them and as his reader and audience, in a slack moment, expect to find them.

Repentance preached everywhere and written about so diligently and, for its time, so convincingly—small wonder that the repentant villain becomes, or remains, a stereotype, especially if he utters an edifyingly repentant last speech to remind the listeners that God's just mercy will triumph, at once viable doctrine and poetic justice. The stereotype repentant sinner is, moreover, remarkably adept in picking up the accent and vocabulary of the time. The cant of Greene's London alleys, the brutal talk of "discontented gentlemen" turned murderer, the scheming soliloquies of the Machiavel, even the accents of courtly love—all of these were easy roles for the villain who rejoices in masquerading as an up-to-date fellow. Always willing to please, he repents easily, thus lending himself to the author's need of a ready and easy way to end a story or a play, witness Proteus's hasty conversion that so outrages modern sensibilities, but is so conveniently and necessarily part of the tradition from which *Two Gentlemen of Verona* derives.

Writers of moral instruction were expected to compose a decent prefatory claim that their works were manuals of virtue. It was all the more necessary for writers of lighter works to elaborate the customary prefatory claim that their books, poems, or plays contained much weighty matter bound up in a way to delight the worthy reader. Prefaces of Elizabethan books are, indeed, so many paraphrases of Horace's *Art of Poetry*, a respectable enough authority. But the purveyors of fiction redoubled their efforts when defending romances. Not that they needed fear for the perdurance of the old form, for it survived quite well; and not until stage and popular romance went down together under the Puritan assault did the charge prevail that such tales were for those who "idly sit down in the Chaire of Ignorance."[10]

In the process of becoming the dominant set of literary

conventions for the late sixteenth and early seventeenth centuries, romance took many forms, appealed to many tastes, profited from many motives. Romances dragged their long and tortuous naratives, on stage as well as in book form, well along into the 1630's, valued even by some of the most discerning Renaissance minds as a way of reaffirming an instructive continuity between their times and a worthy past. We, of course, assume that such naïve specimens as the adventures of Guy of Warwick, a notable savior of women and, according to Samuel Rowland's preface to his 1609 edition, worthy of the favor of "the Honourable Ladies of England," were for the middle and servant class only. And we also assume that Spenser's and Sidney's ideas were only for minds, like theirs, able to comprehend the moral virtues embodied in the Aristotelian magnificent man. These assumptions are at least in partial error. The atmosphere of Arcadia and the Fairy Land of sophisticated romance may have been too rarefied for lower-class mortals. But the reverse is not true. The sophisticated readers of Shakespeare's time evidently delighted, even as their servants did, in the old simple romances and knew the old tales well.

The demand for such stories was insistent from the time of Caxton's shrewdly presenting the *Recuyell of the Historyes of Troy* (1475) as the book most likely to be read in the new printed form. The roster of London stationers from that time on until the mid-seventeenth century is, in effect, a list of publishers of romances for a public consisting of middle-class, even servant-class, readers and also of men of letters and gentlemen, who betray in their correspondence a knowledge of popular romantic narratives. The burgher, his wife and daughter, and the daughter's maid read and believed the romances to be delightful instruction; the lady and gentleman read too, and if they did not believe so implicitly that the romances were delightful instruction, they were sure they could be made so by proper understanding, more refined language, and perhaps a moral or philosophical background imported from the classics. Whatever their preferences, both kinds of readers became as a matter of course necessarily acquainted with the conventions of romance that characterize both popular and literary romance:

the knight serves his lady with unquestioning fidelity; he observes the rituals of the religion of love, and by deeds of prowess shows himself, whether in guise of the Knight o' the Sun or a prince disguised as shepherd, worthy of his lady's favor.

Reading these romances, at best amused by what seems to us the unmotivated and psychologically ridiculous behavior of the stock characters, we exclaim, how unconvincing! But unconvincing to whom? Certainly not to an audience that found the romantic conventions indissolubly wedded to instructive morality. This audience stood always ready to be convinced again, especially if the convention displayed some masterly handling and phrasing so that, while still easily recognizable, it breathed with youthful and optimistic vigor.

Sometimes, to be sure, the gentle reader of the time was put upon by the booksellers, and one must allow for a considerable amount of disingenuousness in the fantastic claims made, for example, by George Whetstone in behalf of his collection of prose romances, *Heptameron of Civill Discourse* (1582), through the perusal of which "the inferiour may learn such rules of Civil Government, as will rase out the Blemish of their Baseness." Naïve, perhaps, but no less so than the claim made for the work of that master of those who know elegance, the arbiter of taste for his generation, John Lyly. His readers could easily "rase out the Blemish of their Baseness" by heeding the mellifluous and passionate declarations of Euphues, who, new man that we suppose he must have seemed to the Elizabethans, nevertheless dwells in a world of familiar romantic conventions. The chief and perhaps the only essential difference between Euphues and the hero of old-fashioned romance is their language. For their motivations and their successes and distresses are all dictated by ancient romantic memories.

But what are we to make of Lyly's trick of importing romance into scenes of actuality by bringing Euphues to England itself, where in a visible London there is a court ruled over by Elizabeth and managed by the astute Burghley? Such touches of romantic glamour existing in a real world made the

refinements of Lyly's book perhaps seem possible of attainment by flesh and blood Englishmen. They could, as it were,
romanticize their very lives.

Nor was the common reader among the Globe audience
denied instruction in the refining code of Euphuism. For Lyly's
works soon became the property of the bourgeoisie through
the reading of Euphues' own words in cheap editions or
through encountering many a pseudo-Euphues in popular imi-
tations, Barnabe Riche's stories, for example, or in the more
expertly done novel of Thomas Lodge, *Rosalynde, Euphues'
Golden Legacie* (1590). Even the indefatigable draper Anthony Munday turned out, in addition to his versions of French
romances, *Zelauto* (1580), a conscious imitation of Lyly's
novels.

The Globe audience knew, moreover, that Euphuism was
more than extravagant refinement in speech. It portrayed, with
its fine speeches and exalted sentiments, a style of life that
earnest readers could imitate, and it thus illustrates the inter-
penetration of life and literature that was assumed by the
Elizabethan mind. To introduce any subject into literature was
immediately to dignify it and to make it morally exemplary.
Thus to put contemporary scenes and characters into obviously elevating stories, as Lyly did in *Euphues and His England* (1580), was to dignify them. The actualities of sixteenth-century England or of English history were dignified
by the association with romantic conventions of fiction, and,
in a complementary way, romance was given verisimilitude
and increased monitory impact by being introduced into history. Romanticized history of this kind was fairly well accepted by the time the playwrights turned their hand to dram-
atizing the chronicles of England.

We can cite again in this regard the prolix Robert Greene,
who, sailing gracefully on all the tides of fashion, cheerfully
romanticized history and made romance historical by employing indifferently the conventions of romance and chronicle as
motivation and narrative framework. What could be more
edifying to a reading public addicted to romance than showing the great and famous men of history experiencing romantic

love too. If the great Cicero loves, we have, as it were, delightful confirmation of the power of ennobling love operating
upon even the sober Roman mind. The novelty of the idea was
not merely pleasing; it was to be taken seriously, because like
any legend about great Rome it must perforce be instructive.
The heroine of Greene's *Ciceronis Amor, Tullies Love* (1589),
speaks from the world of secured convention when she explains to the senate that she loves Tullie because she loves, and
the grave senators must remain content, even as the readers of
all romances must, with the convention that true love fully
possesses the gentle heart at first sight.

Romanticization was not confined to accounts of the past,
however, for if romance could embellish history, it could also
ornament the present and exhibit the congruity of past and
present. To dignify the installation of a member of the Wor-
shipful Company of Fishmongers as Lord Mayor, Anthony
Munday in his pageant, *Chrysanaleia: the Golden Fishing:
or Honour of Fishmongers* (1616), does as his betters have
been doing for several decades and invents what he cannot
find in history. A bit of heartening fiction recounts the exploits
of gallant fishmongers who helped take Jerusalem during the
crusades, and all worthy members of the guild learned anew,
from "actual historical fact," that it was a fishmonger, the
brave Sir William Walworth, who slew Wat Tyler. Even more
impressively does Thomas Heywood, in his *Troia Britanica:
or Great Britaines Troy* (1609), endow his reader and country
with a heroic past and makes every Englishman a participant
in the grand tradition, beginning with the Trojan wanderers
who founded London, the New Troy, and continuing in the
heroic exploits of Sir Francis Drake.

All writers worthy of the publishers' hire had, moreover,
a stock of moralized introductions for the collections of short
stories or tales they pillaged from earlier compilations. These
collections were in turn ransacked by dramatists in search of
a plot. Whetstone, as we have seen, promised his readers benefits, both moral and social, obtainable through perusing his
Heptameron. George Pettie added moral tags to his free adap-
tations of Italian *novelle* published in 1576 as *A Petite Pallace*

of Pettie his Pleasure. So universal were these assurances of benefits derivable from reading this or that bit of literary ephemera that we have to wonder if the Elizabethan common reader paid much attention to them. Probably he took no more than a cursory look to be assured that the customary obeisance had been made and to glean some notion of the contents—in about the same way the present-day common reader glances at a book's dust jacket, skipping over the quoted comments of friendly authors and subservient reviewers, yet all the while reassured by their presence.

All serious readers, however, accepted the historians' claims that past events taught the whole sum of the rewards of virtue and punishments of vice accorded by God to mankind thus far. An extensive account of such events, and one that furnished considerable matter for the stage, was the *Mirror for Magistrates*. Read for three-fourths of a century, it presented history in the form of biographies of noble Englishmen and Romans, linked England with great Rome, and gave proper moral guidance to the readers' judgments. So morally comfortable and so famous a work cannot fail to have affected both theatergoer and dramatist. Instructed about the lives of famous men by these popular verse narratives, the theatergoer heard repeatedly and with approval the reenactments of tragedies attendant upon fortune's inconstancy. The result was that from moralized history and moralized romances, a common body of references had been stored up and already shared in by virtually everyone who came to the Globe.

The Globe audience included representatives of most levels of London society. Equally inclusive was the body of writers who catered to the London public: university wit parading his Latin tags, sonneteer-poet dedicating his work to some noble patron, and at the other extreme, the balladeer and pot-poet dedicating their efforts to the fair ladies of London. The difference between poet and pot-poet, however, was one of degree, not of kind. Both wrote in the same literary tradition, employing the same conventions, and appealing to the common assumption that literature and life were firmly and morally interwoven. The pot-poet, so to speak, worked on the same street as the writer hoping for the patronage of the noble. Barnabe Riche, for example, so inept that Nashe sneered at him as the favorite poet of the barber of Trinity, nevertheless wrote in his *Apolonius and Silla* (1581) a narrative conforming to the demands of romance. Lodge, on the other hand, with all his university training, writes *Rosalynde* with no better command of the essential conventions of plot, narrative, or motivation. His language is smoother, his characters more verbose. This rhetorical distinction is a crucial one, however, as far as contemporary minds like Nashe or Greene are concerned. They maintained that class distinction and educated rhetoric were qualifications for authorship. What right have the lowly to wield the pen? None, say Greene, Lyly, Nashe, and so on. But poor Riche had challenged this literary segregation in his *Allarme to England* (1581) and had established his right to be heard despite his humble origins. This was to the benefit of the drama, for Shakespeare chooses indifferently from the work of the highbrows and that of the bourgeois writers, employing Lodge's *Rosalynde* for *As You Like It* and Riche's *Apolonius and Silla* for *Twelfth Night*.

The modern mind would be hard put to it to say which of Shakespeare's comedies is the better, but would have little hesitation (or thinks it would not) in choosing Lodge over Riche, although perhaps not in appreciative sympathy with either. For Shakespeare both stories were promising; both were grounded on familiar conventions; both raised the fascinating question of what constituted a sound relationship of romance and good morality.

Both bourgeois from the city and young gentleman from the Inns of Court, moreover, relished the high style of *Tamburlaine*, and, their appetites whetted by the rodomontade of *The Spanish Tragedy* and *Titus Andronicus*, welcomed the melodramatic extravagances of *Hamlet*, yet deemed it more than merely another sensational play. Who knows but that a majority of the apprentices as well as of the better sort, if asked their serious opinion, might have preferred Hamlet to Hieronimo and in giving their reasons have revealed at least as much understanding of the drama as a modern audience could state?

Despite the jeers of university wits at lower-class writers whose aspiration ventured beyond the mere concoction of ballads, it was one of their own number and not a pot-poet who gave the most extensive survey of the streets and taverns and slums of London. Robert Greene's literary opportunism inspired his pamphlets of good advice to worthy citizens abroad in the city. In order to avoid urban rascality, he implies, you must be able to recognize it. Therefore, he piles up illustrations in his *Conny-catching* pamphlets of 1591 and 1592. Again, Greene conforms to convention, all the while claiming, as in his repentance pamphlets, to be original and personal; yet the discovery of rascality through confession and boast is at least as old as Chaucer's Pardoner.

These cheerfully frank experts in roguery are doubly lively on stage, for cloaked in the author's respectable intention of improving the audience by salutary warnings against their machinations, they add a note of the contemporary. With their accents of street and wineshop they give rascality a local habitation. Their confessional soliloquies serve the dramatist, moreover, as a primary source of dramatic irony, which confers on the judicious spectator greater knowledge of plot and motive than any character on stage possesses.

This homogeneous quality of Elizabethan literature, springing from that fact that most writers dealt with the same conventions of a coherent literary tradition, is further reinforced by the Elizabethan writers' habit of turning their hands to many lasts. One day pageant-writers, pamphleteers the next, sonneteers or playwrights on another, they employed the same useful conventions indifferently in pamphlets, novels, plays, or set speeches for pageants. When a bourgeois audience of guildsmen was to be flattered, the leading figure of the pageant would be endowed, as happens in Munday's *Chrysanaleia*, with the conventional attributes of the hero of romanticized history. And Heywood, author of *An Apology for Actors*, a comprehensive defense of the drama against Puritan strictures, when he wrote for the less skilled audiences at the Red Bull, exhibited in his *Four Prentices of London* humble hearts engaged in high adventure.

The literary conventions of the books read in considerable number by the Globe audience (or at least offered by the London book trade in considerable numbers to that audience) had, thus, a way of getting into the drama. It is impossible, therefore, to divide the literary tradition of Elizabethan times into dramatic and nondramatic save in those mechanical matters, such as the limitation upon depiction of action, arising from the exigencies of stage production. Even here, the drama was more closely allied with the rest of literature than in the present day. The auditor would expect to find bookish conventions acted out on stage, and even if ill portrayed, would experience on hearing them at least the pleasurable stir of memory. If, however, the conventions were played with a skillful and evocative difference, the spectator would sense a stirring not only of memory but of the spirit too. This perhaps happens in all periods of the drama, but because of the special nature of Shakespeare's literary inheritance and that of his audience there must have been an especially acute awareness of conventions in the minds of both playwright and spectator.

The people who thronged the pathways to the Globe expected, then, to see the familiar, but found that Shakespeare had garbed the familiar in a special rhetoric. Their expectation originated in their education, their experience with literature, and their training in an established theater that had been functioning for two decades by the time Shakespeare sought their approval in his versions of the time-honored *plaudite*.

We cannot know, of course, how diligently the Globe audience conned the books, pamphlets, and plays with which the London booksellers enticed their shillings. Perhaps, like the modern purchaser of paperbounds, the Elizabethan patron of the bookstalls carried his purchases home and ranged them on his shelves merely for present admiration and possible future perusal. Nevertheless, we can know pretty well what was offered the common reader of the latter decades of the sixteenth century in some expectation of his custom. The wide range of that offering is significant, yet not as significant as its remarkable homogeneity originating from the simple fact—so annoying to modern minds—of the Elizabethan habit of regarding literature as virtuous instruction.

Ironically, this expectation that literature could exert such a strong effect was at once the ground for attacks upon the theater and for defenses of the drama. Gosson and Stubbes, chief calumniators of the theater, decried the exhibition of vice on the stage.[11] Nor did they put any trust in the audience's ability to distinguish between right and wrong, for "It is not meet for every man to journey to Corinth." Illustrations of the tangled web of good and evil in men's lives and motives, they distrusted because of the playgoers' lack of moral acumen which might lead them to imitate the bad. The defense of playgoing, however, stemmed from precisely the same assumption that men will imitate what they see portrayed. And Thomas Heywood in his *Apology for Actors* trusts the audience's ethical perceptivity to choose the good for emulation.

Inside the play's own special world and time, and outside the play in the world and time of the audience, the same beliefs held true. The Globe audience and the Globe playwright were united by experience of the written and spoken word as never after in the history of the theater. One need only compare Boswell's nights at the Haymarket to judge the quality of later audiences, or Dickens's remarkable courtship of Thespis, or Arthur Miller's gibe, reported by Kenneth Tynan, that Broadway audiences demand sops and trifles and he will have no part of such degrading traffic.[12] Not since the Athenians in the theater of Dionysos judged Sophocles to have won the prize has there been so literate an audience or one so well equipped to test a playwright's mettle as that which applauded Shakespeare's plays at the Globe.

IV

The Upstart Crow

An intending playwright nowadays on arriving in the city takes a room and communes with himself. Brooding on his troubles with home, school, and society, he is loath to give an approving picture of the time, and his craft of condemnation is perhaps the sign of a deteriorating age; Juvenal displaces Horace. The young Shakespeare, actor of minor parts for the Lord Chamberlain's men, and engaged from time to time in the "reversion" of old plays, was not one to brood publicly over his troubles with home, school, and whatever establishment oppressed him. Nor was he merely an impartial observer of the actualities of his time, painstakingly recording the play of light and shade on the landscape of the present. He dearly wanted success, and for him, to use today's idiom, the price was right.

In order to attain success, however, he had to serve an apprenticeship in pleasing a rather exacting audience, one that became increasingly demanding as its skill and experience grew. The trade in which he was apprenticed exacted, moreover, a self-conscious loyalty to tradition, and viewed itself as an important part of a society in which there was as much of the medieval, in custom and inclination, as of anything that was felt to be new, therefore better. The badge that he and his fellows were entitled to wear, signifying the livery of the Lord Chamberlain, allowed them a place in that society.[1] It was as dear to them as any possession. They felt it seemly to be thus integrated into society as men of quality, to whom respect and honor were due. Their craft, moreover, was guided by ideas and practices that had been cherished for a long time. Although modern scholars conscientiously record this evidence of the importance of tradition and convention in the society and theater of the time, they somehow minimize its importance by depicting Shakespeare as a superlative genius adventuring beyond conventions to assert mastery not only over his age but all time. But Shakespeare worked in a theater quite convinced of the soundness of its received ideas and beliefs. It had, furthermore, a satisfactory number of stock characters, plots and themes, a generous supply of universally approved metaphors, and a generally applauded moralistic intention. His apprenticeship, then, consisted of acquiring the mastery of these and reworking them into successful plays.

This period of apprenticeship I determine for the sake of a more concise presentation to last through 1598,[2] when the move to the Globe theater marks a definite change into a period of unquestioned mastery in which there is only one comparative failure, *Troilus and Cressida*. The pre-Globe period, however, sees plays that are excellent journeyman work but none of them masterpieces. This seems a long period of apprenticeship for one customarily termed a genius, and of course there is a difference between the skills apparent in *The Comedy of Errors* and those that mark *Romeo and Juliet*. But what I am chiefly concerned with in this section is Shakespeare's management of dramatic conventions and his way of transferring the conventions from nondramatic to dramatic settings, in short, his manner of filling out what Harbage calls the "cartoon" which the source afforded him.[3] This process is chiefly one of shaping the literary and dramatic conventions to his ends, in other words, the daily manage of his craft, in which he gradually acquires mastery in the period 1591–98. For whatever the coincidence is worth, this is the traditional seven years' span for apprenticeship.

The judicious spectator at the new Globe in 1599 knew that when Shakespeare's play was on, with Burbage, Heminge, and Condell in the cast, he was seeing the best that the Bankside season could offer. Francis Meres would certainly have said so, and it is a further coincidence that his *Palladis Tamia* (1598), in which he places Shakespeare in the first rank of contemporary dramatists, attests to Shakespeare's successful apprenticeship in the years before the opening of the Globe. The plays from this period mentioned by Meres form a body of drama ranging from the comparatively inept *Two Gentlemen of Verona* to the smoothly popular *Romeo and Juliet*. Nevertheless, they exhibit a more or less consistent use of the standard conventional themes and situations.

No dramatist or writer of the Renaissance, for instance, any more than a medieval writer of fiction, could hope to please without having become skillful in the narration of courtly romance. As I have suggested in the preceding chapters, Shakespeare and his contemporaries would have learned the romantic conventions in their very schoolbooks—witness the exercises in composition prescribed by the Erasmian schoolmasters of England—and in all literature, popular as well as aristocratic, the conventions held full sway relatively unchanged since their formulations by medieval romancers like Chrétien de Troyes.

Small wonder, then, that Shakespeare first mastered so flexible, pliant, and adaptable dramatic media as the conventions of the love-game comedy. Greater wonder that he should have remained loyal to them in his mature pieces and employed them to give substance to his last plays. But, it might be objected, if these conventions were so well known and widely used, ready to the hand of any carpenter of stage spectacles, was it not Shakespeare's verse that made his plays more than old journalism refurbished? Did he not turn out superior plays in spite of the conventional nature of the material his pen set to work on? The point of view suggested by these objections is a "magic, pure magic!" attitude, which implies that Shakespeare's wizardry is instinctive, not calculated. His verse in this view covers up a thousand flaws of loose plotting and tired stereotype characters, somehow bringing the shabbiest bit of stock situation or characterization to warm-blooded life.

No one will gainsay any interpretation of Shakespeare's art that urges an understanding appreciation of the verse. But it makes a difference, after all, what it is that the verse brings to life. Shakespeare paid close attention to what he said as well as how he said it, and in his use of the conventional material revealed a calculation that is, like his command of verse, a hallmark of his genius.

During this period of apprentice and journeyman work at the Theatre in Holywell, he tends to use the conventions explicitly. He discovers, moreover, the dramatic feasibility of first testing the conventions by mockery and contradiction and then reaffirming their soundness. Take, for example, the court of love and the school of love, situations certainly not novel either for Shakespeare or for his audience. In *Love's Labour's Lost*, we find that the court of love is the framework of the entire play. Note also that this play has no generally acknowledged set of analogues or sources. We must deduce, then, that Shakespeare's pen, freed from obligation to any earlier story or play, writes the same kind of play and employs the same conventions that it does when following the lead of the tradition embodied in some source story or play.

The situation at the opening of *Love's Labour's Lost* must have seemed to contemporary audiences a curious mixture of the well known and novel. For even without the benefit of a modern director's delusion that an Elizabethan play is enhanced by a surprise opening scene filled with outlandish costumes, circus stunts, and music-hall turns, it should be apparent that Navarre and his companions are engaged in flouting tradition and custom. They are parodying the court of love and its concomitant school of love of the old tradition. Their academe is a negation of the school of love, and their court a court of nonlove. No *débats d'amour* take these young men's minds from their studies, and they swear to be votaries not to love but to love's enemy.

As any beginning dramatist must know, or learn, to show characters engaged in flouting a familiar code of beliefs or involved in a familiar situation gone awry creates dramatic apprenhension in the audience. From long acquaintance Shakespeare's audience knows that rebels against love's power are always punished, converted, and chastised into penitence. The more presumptuous Navarre, Longaville, Dumaine, and Berowne show themselves in their flouting of love, the more severe will be their correction.

Correction is not long in appearing, for as soon as the

princess and her ladies arrive, a safe return to the tenets of the tradition is promised. But it is not an easy correction. To the strange court of nonlove maintained by Navarre, the princess and her ladies come as petitioners—another convention inverted, for petitioners are ordinarily distraught lovers in search of redress at the court of love. The only recourse for the rejected ladies is to lay siege to the unfriendly court, whereupon the youths' resistance proves feeble indeed. Renouncing their vows to false gods, they enlist under the banners of Cupid once more and expect confidently to be welcomed at the princess's court, that is, the court of love.

It is not as easy as the youths expect, however, for their lives have been riddled with heresy, and the cure must be as drastic as the disease was severe. The climax of the play depends, fittingly, upon the religion-of-love metaphor. For there are many heresies noised about in this strange Platonized and Puritanized society of Navarre's court where the princess can ruefully say to the forester's awkward attempt at compliment:

> See, see, my beauty will be saved by Merit!
> O heresy in fair, fit for these days!
> [IV.i.21–22]

According to the old religion of love, there could be no question of beauty's merit; beauty should be venerated, not judged, tried, or tested according to its moral deserts. New doctrine pervades this world of Navarre and his heretical companions. They should be engaged in the pious works of love: service of fair ladies, veneration and courtship. Instead they have become votaries of nonlove, which amounts, in the vein of the sonnets, to nonlife. These sinners, however, attain grace by recanting and, as it were, by contrition and confession. Absolved by their several goddesses, who impose as penance a year of performing the corporal acts of mercy, they can expect that at the end of the penitential time the ladies will grant them "mercy."

As far as narrative, plot, and characterization go, *Love's Labour's Lost* is, by comparison with Shakespeare's later comedies, pretty thin stuff. Modern producers try to make it robust by introducing gadgetry—motor cars, for example, and chorus girls. In a way, they are right in doing so. For if producer and audience do not know what the play is really about, they might as well enjoy the superficialities of noise and display. Actually, the play could be produced so as to instruct even a modern audience in the courtly code as well as to entertain, so precise and pleasant is its following of the pattern. The play consists not of character and story but primarily of a reversal of a conventional pattern, followed by a pleasing righting of the topsy-turvy world of Navarre, and a final reaffirmation of the tradition.

It is very easy to misread Shakespeare's use of convention and to side with the mockers of love—and thus to make nonsense of the play. When the ladies command the young men to renounce all pleasures for a year, the modern reader or auditor, not knowing the convention with the same appreciative sympathy of the mind of the early 1590's, is tempted to see a reproach of what he thinks is the essential falsity of the love game, a judgment he readily ascribes to Shakespeare also. He finds encouragement for his view in Berowne's resolve to court "in russet yea's and honest kersey no's," which seems to be a manly rejection of pretense. Actually, Berowne's resolution is prompted not by disgust with the courtly conventions but by his unsuccessful attempt at courtly wooing. He is only temporarily discouraged. No more than the sport enjoyed by the princess and her companions at the showing up of the youths is his discomfiture an undermining of the tradition. The ladies, moreover, are simply asserting their privilege, given them in the old dispensation, of deciding what to do with the very lives of the men who court them. The lady has, of course, the prerogative of demanding proof of her lover's worthiness. Thus, Berowne will be worthier for his year spent in performing the corporal acts of mercy; besides, he receives condign punishment for having so flagrantly defied the god of love.

In apologies for the love-game comedy, which is what the early comedies amount to, a devil's advocate must, for the sake of dramatic effectiveness, have a voice. But let it not be too persuasively effective lest the play go awry and the disman-

tling of the court of love be deemed the instructive aim. Fortunately, the tradition itself allows, even demands, that such
voices be heard, voices that are either scoffers at love, convenient villains fortunately of not much power to hurt, who in
stereotyped fashion hate all young lovers because they hate
love itself; or they are clowns and fools whose ineptness affords the audience the innocent amusement of learning how
not to behave. With the resultant comforting sense of superiority, we know we too are on the side of witty gentility and
refinement.

In *Love's Labour's Lost* there is no villain to plot against
lovers' meetings; only the prospect of lovers' partings saddens
us, and these, we know, will not be for long. In the meantime,
we have our amusement, even as do the aristocratic youths in
the make-believe court of love. Costard's wooing of his lady
affords sport for his betters, among whom we count ourselves.
Yet Costard's susceptibility to the wiles of Eve's daughters is
an effective subversion of the king's proclamation banishing
all women from the court. "Such is the simplicity of man to
hearken after the flesh," he confesses on his own behalf, thus
lulling the foolish young gentlemen into a sense of security.
They cannot imagine any kinship with the hapless Costard,
yet they fall and just as surely. But theirs is, of course, a return
to the correct deportment decreed by the school of love from
which Costard is as firmly barred as from the king's Platonic
academe. *Fin amour* is for gentlefolk only, and for the wellborn and well-bred. This requirement also excludes Don
Armado, compounded from braggart warrior and melancholiac, whose treason against his oath of loyalty to the king's
academe consists in his being "converted" to the love of a
country wench. This is, of course, double treason, for country
wenches have no place in the aristocratic court of love.

Nevertheless, Don Armado is a consistently drawn character. His lament apes that of his betters: "If drawing my
sword against the humor of affection would deliver me from
the reprobate thought of it, I would take Desire prisoner, and
ransom him to any French courtier for a new devised curtsy"
(I.ii.63–67). Armado knows his love literature; he recognizes

the menace of Desire, that unruly inhabitant of the court of love allegory. He also knows that the true lover must receive instruction in the school of love, where, however, the diminutive Moth, expert Cupid that he is, finds the Don a "negligent student." Thus, the court of love, the school of love, the religion of love of the main plot are all parodied, item by item, by the characters of the subplot. Shakespeare is evidently learning how to temper his jest so as to set off the serious business of the subject jested about, thus bringing a fully developed conventional situation into sharper focus by means of the judiciously created tension that puts under great stress but does not rupture the traditional form and pattern.

The court of love continues for Shakespeare a most effective dramatic instrument throughout his dramatic career. Although he will not again develop it with the explicitness of *Love's Labour's Lost,* he will use it repeatedly as a way of managing denouements. It provides a setting for judgments given by moral authority, thus sorting well with the expected instructiveness of Elizabethan literature. Such judgments resolve questions of love and honor (as in *All's Well that Ends Well*), punish those who have transgressed against charity and love (*Measure for Measure*), and reward those who exercise gracious forgiveness of repentant sinners against love's commandments (*Cymbeline*).

Love's Labour's Lost is a full-dress and skillful dramatization of the major conventions of romantic comedy. But even in other plays of this early period which are not adapted from romantic stories, the courtly conventions play an important part. The dramatically promising method of delineating and developing character by having a youth become a convert to love and, finally, a rewarded devotee begins in what is almost certainly the first comedy Shakespeare wrote altogether by himself, *The Comedy of Errors* (1590). Derived from the Plautine model, it is, unremarkably, what one would expect of a clever student of the drama as taught and perhaps acted in the grammar school. The cleverness consists, for the most part, in doubling the intrigue, a device sufficiently ingenious to add a modicum of interest for an audience probably quite familiar with Plautus's *Menaechmi*. But Shakespeare even at this early stage seems to have been so wholeheartedly committed to the conventions of romance that he employs them as a more interesting way of complicating and adapting his source.

In order to exploit to the utmost the comic situation of lovers wooing at cross purposes, love at first sight, that is, instantaneous conversion to the religion of love, commits Antipholus of Syracuse, the wanderer in Ephesus, to a lifelong, ennobling devotion to his lady. Unfortunately, his lady is Luciana, who believes him to be her own brother-in-law and thinks his pledges of love the utterings of a mind vilely deranged. Emboldened by the fervor that the religion of love inspires, however, Antipholus protests his regeneration by the power of love. "Are you a god?" he asks,

> Would you create me anew?
> Transform me, then, and to your power I'll yield.
> [III.ii.39–40]

This admixture of the religion of love and classic farce with the resultant transformation of love farce into the romance of marriage exemplifies the English habit of freely transferring conventions from one decorum to another, a practice condemned by Italian and French classicists but found profitably expedient by Elizabethan dramatists. Sometimes this stratagem operates successfully for Shakespeare; sometimes with dramatically unfortunate results as in *The Merchant of Venice;* but never with dullness or flatness. Thus, in *The Comedy of Errors* the conventional view of the romance of marriage is defended, to add one more touch of paradox, not by the happily married woman but by Luciana, the happily unmarried woman. Again, at the end of the play, the romance of marriage is given authoritative voice by the abbess, who speaks of the proper, orderly relationships of marriage, the ultimate lesson in the school of love, and one employed by the Elizabethan writers of romance with the full approval of Elizabethan readers. When, therefore, the Dromios end the play with the classic *plaudite*, they are asking the audience to applaud not merely the cleverness of Plautus reworked but the reassuring spectacle of greater instruction added to amusement. The abbess is appropriately the adjudicator of the dissensions of romance that are so neatly resolved in a court of love wherein virtue is defined according to the tenets of the religion of love.

A Midsummer Night's Dream (1595), however, employs the court-of-love convention as beginning and end. A convention ideally suited to the restoration of characters to what they had been before mischance or evil overtook them, it affords the rediscovery of a lost happiness rather than a progress into a new and better state. The stately nuptials of Theseus and Hippolyta, of course, make of the court of Athens a perfect court of love, with the duke and his consort the judges of the *débat d'amour*.

The questions debated in the traditional court of love usually concerned constancy in love. From the time of the *Concilium in Monte Romarici* in the twelfth century, writers had sought to stimulate interest in their stories by appealing to the readers' judgment, which they then attempted to sway by adducing examples of constant lovers, for constancy in love is the whole duty of the votary in love's religion. Demetrius has won one lady's love and then abandoned her, thus deserving Lysander's accusation, "This spotted and inconstant man." The two youths stand before the duke, ready for his judgment as lord of love. But what judgment is it possible to mete to those who, under the spell of Puck's charm have loved and erred and loved again? Surely it must be, as Theseus wisely judges, to restore the morally and conventionally correct situation that existed before the play began.

A liking for complexity begins to affect Shakespeare's dealing with sources during this period and guides his most mature dramatic proceedings: one conventional plot situation or set of characters or intrigue seems to call for a subplot, usually involving a similar theme from the same tradition as the main plot and providing some kind of comparison or contrast. This method appears first in romances because the tradition itself calls for humorous parody. But Shakespeare finds it equally serviceable in tragedy and history. Subplots constructed from the romance tradition provide sets of characters to mock and jest at the expense of the main plot. Thus with *A Midsummer Night's Dream:* the court of love governed by Theseus and Hippolyta in complete harmony and assurance evokes a court of nonlove, even as in *Love's Labour's Lost* the king's court of nonlove was at first countered by and finally overturned by the court of love. The discordancies of the court of Oberon and Titania provide this contrast, and when the fairy monarchs, who should be lording it over happy unions and love's true encounters, fall out, all nature goes awry.

One cannot speak of the court of love, however, without noticing also the associated convention of the religion of love. A deliberate irony marks the use of these interlocked conventions in *A Midsummer Night's Dream*, for the laws of Athens as recapitulated by Theseus in the opening scene in the ducal court decree that the unwilling or disobedient maiden spend a lifelong, compelled devotion to the religion of nonlove as a votary of Diana rather than of Venus.

The oaths of fidelity that fall so easily from the lips of votaries in the religion of love furnish opportunities for verbal displays, which the apprentice Shakespeare shapes into litanies of love. In these early plays, action stops while youth becomes eloquent in protestation. In *A Midsummer Night's Dream*, Hermia speaks her vows at length simply to promise to keep her tryst with Lysander. Her promises are in effect a litany of the saints of love, with, however, some curious additions. For although she swears, most properly, by "Cupid's bow," she also invokes the false oaths of deceitful lovers. The ear of the connoisseur would delight in the irony, whereas the unwary would be lulled by the conventional beginning of Hermia's speech. The same sort of litany, moreover, is used with musically telling effect as a most engaging prelude to the reunion of true lovers at Belmont, as Lorenzo and Jessica together recite the litany of the saints of love.

That love ennobles is a truism whose validity is assumed not only in *Love's Labour's Lost*, but also in *The Comedy of Errors*, and tested again in *Romeo and Juliet*. It is also subject to the test of parody in the misfortunes of Costard and Armado in *Love's Labour's Lost*, and in vivid demonstration in *A Midsummer Night's Dream*, as Bottom with most gentlemanly and modest behavior assumes the role of Titania's cavalier. Shakespeare never lets his low characters stray too far from their proper station, however. Their congeniality submits cheerfully to restrictions imposed by conventions, and they do not overstep the bounds of decorum. Humble folk, both he and she, remain that and are not metamorphosed into eloquent speakers of courtly language, as they are in some other dramatists' careless handling of the tradition. Bottom himself knows the rules of the school of love, but his language remains his own. "A lover is more condoling," he advises his fellows, but neither he nor any other amiable rustic or clown in Shakespeare's play takes himself seriously as a conscious lover on the level of the gentlefolk.

Whereas the court-of-love convention returns characters to a lost happiness, the school of love changes their natures so that they grow in grace by learning the commandments of love and absorbing the virtue resulting from the practice of the rituals of the religion of love. The youths of *Love's Labour's Lost* become better for their being dislodged from the court of nonlove and experiencing transformation into devotees of love. Benedick and Beatrice are both tricked into conning the lessons of the school of love. And Valentine and Proteus learn the lessons of virtue that are basic in love's curriculum. The most obvious use of the pattern of the school-of-love convention, however, which exploits the farcical possibilities of upsetting the known conventions and then setting them right again is in *The Taming of the Shrew* (1597).

The Shrew is a play divided. The courting of Bianca derives from a known source, and the wooing and winning of Kate seems to be Shakespeare's own story (for the relationship of the anonymous *A Shrew* to *The Shrew* remains a most unsettled quetsion). Pure invention, however, would be too strong a term for the taming-of-Kate intrigue, for the playwright's purpose limits his choices of character and situation to aspects of the tradition that will help set off the other intrigue of the winning of Bianca. Suppose, for the moment, that

Shakespeare had no specific model. Could he not make the standard wooing story, adopted from Ariosto's *I Suppositi*, more interesting (and marketable too because it combines the novel, the conventional, and the instructive) by adding a topsy-turvy wooing story that would be a school of love not for the man but for the lady; in which the lady, having been schooled, would in turn instruct others, presumably the better scholars, in what they had not learned well, that is the popular, morally instructive relationships of the romance of marriage. Better than that, he could employ the school of love in the serious plot as model for the parody of the school enacted in the farce plot. All kinds of possibilities suggest themselves—far beyond the talents or imagination of diligent George Gascoigne when he adapted Ariosto's play.

Shakespeare evidently cared less about fidelity to the classical farce aspects of Gascoigne's play than about the motivations inherent in the love-game comedy. Lucentio, trading places with his servant Tranio, assumes the role of wooer in romance who proclaims himself servant to his lady in order to win her. His task is not altogether easy, however, even though he shows himself an adept in the art of courtship. What, for instance, should be his disguise so as to outwit tyrannical fathers, both his and his lady's? Naturally—since the school of love is the convention ready to hand—a schoolmaster. How patly it comes off. True, Hortensio disguised as a music master provides strenuous competition. Music does indeed have charm, but in the school of love in which Lucentio finds Bianca a forward pupil, the schoolmaster has the insurmountable advantage of giving out assignments; and it is his prerogative to assess his pupil's progress.

Kate makes a remarkable candidate for instruction in that branch of the school of love conducted by Petruchio, who improvises a course leading to a mastery of the bourgeois ideal of the romance of marriage, a quite orthodox and proper conclusion for so madcap an instructor. Petruchio's instruction is devious, however, for, assuming the role of braggart and fantastic, he makes the orthodox school of love, in which the lady gracefully accepts honorable devotion, seem so much more attractive to Kate than her willful independence that she must regret not having earlier lived by its rules. Exhausted by having her every whim taken literally in a travesty of the courtly relationship of mistress and servant-wooer, she gladly gives Petruchio mastery and obediently recites the instructive credo of domesticity that nevertheless assumes romance as prelude.

Unfortunately, the importance of the courtly conventions in *The Taming of the Shrew* and the other early comedies goes, for the most part, unrecognized. Far from being validated, it is felt, the conventions are somehow undermined. This view results in lamentable displacements of dramatic emphases, rendering, for example, Petruchio's corrective measures merely bewildering, noisy slapstick. The modern producer would deal more justly with the play if he knew better what was being made sport of and what, at the end of the play, was being condoned.

The changes in character in *The Shrew* are, except for Kate, matters of adopting or discarding disguises of costume. The disguise of hypocrisy employed by characters in other of these early plays, however, serves better as a source of dramatic irony, and in romance such a disguise is doubly useful. In *The Two Gentlemen of Verona*, for example, so effective is the disguise of hypocrisy that modern critics have been taken in and have read the entire play as a travesty of the courtly tradition, terming it with curious illogic not a good play in itself but so effective an attack upon romance as to disable the whole tradition—a remarkable achievement, if it were true, for so young a dramatist as Shakespeare was in 1594. Not even Robert Greene in the well-known passage in his *Groatsworth of Wit* accused Shakespeare of dealing so shockingly as to discard and ruin the plumage he borrowed from the established playwrights. Yet this is the judgment on Shakespeare's use of convention made by those who, like Hereward Price, would interpret Shakespeare's romantic comedies as a deliberate campaign of moral and aesthetic renovation of the Elizabethan theater. An attractive point of view, this, for it makes

Shakespeare a participant in the modern censure of the courtly
conventions as an inheritance of implausibilities that through
long repetition had become silly, even dangerous, for they deflect attention from certain stern realities of the relationship
of sex and society.

Unfortunately for this point of view, *Two Gentlemen*, far
from undermining the courtly tradition, is a masterpiece of
handling conventional material, of testing the conventions so
as to send the audience away confirmed in its faith in the
soundness of the beliefs symbolized in the formalities of the
courtly code. The oft-rehearsed commandments of love, for
example, govern the language and the conduct of the youths.
Proteus—suspicious name—obeys the code of amatory address
at the beginning, and his lady, Julia, though sympathetically
aware of his love distress, is obliged by the code to reject his
advances. But secretly, as the audience is privileged to observe, she too is love-sick. No need to rehearse for the audience
the ensuing well-known behavior of the lover so as to characterize Proteus, for the audience can tell at a word what stock
character Shakespeare intends us to understand. But it adds
a bit of interest to have Julia depart from the code's requirements as she, in private, pieces together Proteus's letter, which
she had earlier torn in a mood of conformity to the tradition's
bidding the lady be disdainful of the lover's first missive.

It has been said that Shakespeare put too much character
in Julia for the story.[4] Julia does indeed have character, but
her character is a response to the exigencies of the story, and
not something separate. For Julia is an excellent example of
one of Shakespeare's methods of "creating character." The conventional pattern of the story requires that in public she utter
certain sentiments. In her soliloquies, however, and when she
is disguised, she can comment ironically on those requirements. But she does not want to destroy the convention; she
wants it reestablished for her own happiness and for the sake
of Proteus. This reestablishment of the conventional relationships of the lovers is the proper conclusion of the story and
unites, not separates, character and story. Julia comments, for
instance, on the anomaly of her situation when in disguise she

takes service as page to Proteus and becomes servant of him who, according to the tradition, should be her "servant":

> I am my master's true-confirmed love,
> But cannot be true servant to my master,
> Unless I prove false traitor to myself.
>
> [IV.iv.110–12]

Note that she wants to and finally does regain the status of "my master's true-confirmed love." This seems to me not one of the "realistic touches of motive" by which, it is asserted, Shakespeare brings a character to life. It is, rather, a touch of irony that reinforces, not dispels, the conventional quality of both story and character.

Proteus's character is likewise ironically complicated. Expert on the behavior of lovers, he poses as a master in the school of love to the foolish Thurio, that unzestful lover, counseling him to employ pen and voice in a better progress of his suit by writing complaints to his lady and singing serenades beneath her window. The play is crowded, however, with experts in the art of wooing. Valentine, converted scoffer at love, also turns instructor, advising the duke to woo his supposititious lady with "persistent reminders of love." Secrecy is essential to the school of love, and the duke should "resort to her by night," says Valentine, offering "an engine" for the purpose, a rope ladder, which he can provide at once. This practical application of the lesson of courtship proves Valentine's undoing, however, and is a turning point in the action. The duke, opening Valentine's cloak, discovers the ladder that Valentine is at the very moment carrying toward Silvia's balcony. Thus is the novice instructor in love's stratagems discomfited by the cynical duke, for whom love is but "a figure trenched in ice." This sounds not at all like giving the age a purge; it is simply a device of comedy. After all, Valentine's suit is genuine, and the duke is merely a figure of disbelieving, crabbed age. Who among the audience would choose to be of the duke's inclining?

The audience also chooses between Proteus and Valentine, becoming itself involved in this *débat d'amour*. Valentine, repentant sinner against love, has made his *mea culpa* and has become a votary. He is, as it were, saved. But Proteus, resolving on treachery, like a notable sinner invokes the deity:

> Love, lend me wings to make my purpose swift
> As thou hast lent me wit to plot this drift.
>
> [II.iv.42–43]

Once his treachery has been discovered, however, Proteus repents, confesses, and is given absolution. Thus is the full ritual of the religion of love acted out.

The test of the sinner's repentance, however, in real life and in tragedy as well as in the fancy of romantic legend, is whether he will willingly give up that which through sin he has won. This was the crux of Claudius's life and Macbeth's, and Proteus's too. Proteus, therefore, if the religion-of-love metaphor is to be preserved, must be cured of sin. His cure must be more than lip service. We need a demonstration of faith, not a merely verbal repentance, to test the conventionally remorseful sinner—and to impress the audience with the playwright's daring to risk the entire tradition as well as the effectiveness of the play itself. Mere words of penitence from Proteus might satisfy the moral issue but would certainly be a lackluster acknowledgment of the convention. Therefore, Valentine's fantastic offer of Silvia to the man from whose threats of violence he has just rescued her should be regarded as a suspenseful *tour de force*, of the same kind as Richard's wooing of Lady Anne.

Proteus's violation of the code of honor in friendship and in love has almost won for him the Lady Silvia. Receiving a check, he might feign repentance. Valentine's offer is, however, so searching a test that it must for a certainty reveal the genuineness of Proteus's repentance. Were he insincere, off he could go with the prize—even as, perhaps, the critics who jeer at the play ("There are no gentlemen in Verona!") would have him do. Fortunately, Proteus's repentance is as sincere as it is instantaneous. And why should it not be? The courtly tradition expects such changes in man's moral nature. So does religion, and, for that matter, so does psychology. If, therefore, we have accepted Valentine's quick conversion to love and Proteus's rapid change of mind about his ladies, we ought not boggle at the changes of the last act. They are consonant with the tradition; they reaffirm the soundness of the tradition; and they reflect the faith of the age in those soul-nourishing qualities of love and honor. There are indeed gentlemen in Verona after all. What we need is more skill in keeping up with Shakespeare's deft use, even in this early play, of the narrative speed and accuracy of characterization permitted by conventions whose fancifulness is, moreover, rendered dramatically convincing by other aspects of the tradition, those down-to-earth comical love imbroglios like Launce's that by deflecting harmful laughter make the principal intrigue more romantically credible.

Madeleine Doran in her *Endeavors of Art* dislikes the play almost as much as Hereward Price does. Story and character, she asserts, are at odds, and though the story requires that every Jack must have his Jill, "we protest" at the fickle Proteus's having Julia.[5] Although Doran and Price find it hard to forgive Proteus, we must realize that the conventions of the play require that Julia do so. Nor does Northrop Frye, who rightly insists that conventions are structural elements in Shakespeare's plays, see that this scene is itself essential to the play's structure. According to him, Valentine, after rescuing Silvia from an attempted rape, amiably makes a present of her to Proteus. A director who encouraged the actor playing the role of Valentine to be amiable at this point should be cashiered at once as guilty of not understanding the true import of the scene. There should be firmness in Valentine's tone, not amiability. For Shakespeare is actually very nicely balancing the conventional material of both story and character and has Proteus undergo and pass a rigorous test indeed. Frye, who points out the lapses of critics who refuse to accept the conventions of a Shakespearean play, seems in this instance perhaps to have erred even as Doran and Price.[6]

The audience, furthermore, is tested by having put to it this question: can it forgive Proteus? If it has been convinced of the validity of Julia's characterization, and if that characterization includes the question of whether she will or will not forgive Proteus, it must either applaud her decision or admit to having erred in its earlier sympathetic judgment of her and dismiss her and the whole play along with Proteus as not worth any mature person's attention. This is the kind of dilemma that audiences are forever being faced with when they pay close attention to Shakespeare's characterizations, and we often discover that what at first seems a flaw in characterization or plot turns out to be a necessary part of the play's structure. The way out of this particular dilemma is, I suggest, to follow the lead of the tradition and do as Shakespeare bids: accept Proteus's repentance as well as Julia's forgiveness of him, rejoice with the right-minded that one more brand has been saved from the burning, and enjoy a play that is remarkably well made.

Those who make of Shakespeare an iconoclast find *Much Ado about Nothing* an even better instrument of demolition than *Two Gentlemen,* and they assume that Shakespeare intended it to be such. They cite as the major case in point what they term Benedick's renunciation of the insincerities of romance and his consequent dedication to forthrightness. Benedick is, to be sure, a more sympathetic character than Berowne or either of the gentlemen of Verona. When, therefore, Benedick declares, "I cannot woo in festival terms," the modern critic (Donald Stauffer, for example) cheers him on, assuming that Shakespeare, evincing a growing dissatisfaction with the conventions of courtly romance, frees Benedick to win his lady with forthright, sincere address, thus becoming a better man, worthy of our approval.[7] And Frye says of the young lovers that their real feelings are allowed to break free of their verbal straitjackets.[8]

Quite contrary to such interpretations Benedick is not rejecting any convention at all. He is regretting his inability to be the Renaissance wooer, accomplished in word as well as act, at once poet and man of deeds. He has tried to conform to the manners decreed by the code of love. He has attempted to compose sonnets and regrets the mediocrity of his meters. Like Berowne, he is a figure of comedy, not an inconoclast sent by Shakespeare to hammer down the idols of romantic memory. He is, moreover, when we look at him closely, a thoroughly conventional figure, compounded of cheerful mocker at love and converted scoffer at love, figures wholly within the tradition. Shakespeare adapts the conventions to his dramatic use; he is learning to employ them in making novel and interesting combinations; he does not war against them, for he knows that without the courtly conventions there could be no mocking Benedicks. He wants to go on exploiting such humorous attacks upon conventions, attacks which are themselves conventional.

One wonders, moreover, if those who rejoice in what they take to be Benedick's turning to forthrightness and honesty in wooing really think that the love-game comedy, especially in its employment of the metaphor of the religion of love, is dishonest and lacks forthrightness. By this token, anyone who swears by the god of love is suspect, but he who is blunt and direct, whose wooing is russet yeas and nays, is to be trusted. Shakespeare uses both characterizations, of course. The fantastic votary is an object of fun, but we notice that in Shakespeare's comedy, honest youths who begin as witty mockers at love and not fantastics end as sincere professors of the true faith in the god of love. In tragedy also, the scoffer at the substance as well as the wording of the old faith, be it the religion of love or belief in the natural correspondences, is likely to be an adherent of evil, and his soliloquized credo of rejection of conventional belief is a hint to the audience to be on guard against his hypocritical villainy. Not that the burgher in the audience, convinced after seeing one of Shakespeare's comedies of the soundness of the courtly way of love, will hasten homeward to proclaim to his wife his faith in the god of love so as to prove himself not a rascal. He probably will not. But in the theater he will find characters more to his liking if they are faithful adherents of honest love.

The mocker of unskillful or extravagant use of the language of the love game, however, ingratiates himself with the audience by evoking its admiration of his sound judgment and good rhetoric. For mastery of felicitous speech is an enviable attainment, as any Elizabethan would acknowledge. Mastery of idioms, moreover, requires a prior esthetic faith in the subject spoken of. Moral commitment may or may not be involved, though it is hard to see how in the long run the two can remain separate. In Shakespeare's dramas, at any rate, the youth who learns the eloquence of love is also called upon to act for his professed faith. Thus, *Much Ado* is an ingenious examination of the validity of the phrases of the love-game comedy, testing its metaphors of the religion of love, the school of love, the feudal service of love, and, furthermore, fully exploiting the possibilities of characterization afforded by the tradition's endowing the lady with power over the very life of her lover.

In *Much Ado*, written toward the end of the "apprentice" period, we observe also the way in which Shakespeare is learning to put the audience's familiarity with the ramifications of the courtly tradition to use. He trusts his audience to recognize the conventions and does not have to spell out the whole pattern of wooing and winning before setting his counterplot in motion. Thus the pattern of the love game is indicated but not played out in the main plot. The wooing and winning of Hero is, for example, conducted for the most part offstage. The existence of true love having been expeditiously affirmed early in the play, we can readily believe in Hero's integrity, the intensity of Claudio's anguish, and Don Pedro's indignation.

This involvement of honor is a moral appeal, constraining the audience to participate actively in judging the characters' actions and motives. The audience cannot help responding with attitudes and beliefs summoned from a moral consciousness stimulated by the appeal to an approved tradition. Does Shakespeare reject any part of this tradition? On the contrary he draws very carefully upon it so as to give greater impact to Beatrice's command to Benedick: "Kill Claudio." Command is the proper term, for it is not merely the request of a woman made desperate by the wrongs done her friend. The conventional attitudes toward honest wooing, love and honor, honor and friendship account for the heightened effect of Beatrice's words.

Her command is, therefore, hardly meaningful without reference to the courtly code. Unless we see it as part of that code, we cannot view it otherwise than as Shakespeare's sacrificing dramatic credibility and consistency of characterization in order to surprise his audience. Surprised the audience is, of course, but at the just application and shrewd use of this part of the feudal metaphor of the relationships of lover and lady. Heroes of romance may not question the justness of their ladies' commands; Lancelot never allowed himself to think that the whims of the capricious Guenevere were sometimes excessive when, for example, as Chrétien de Troyes narrates it in *Le Comte de la Charette*, he willingly subjects himself to the mockery of the villagers by riding in a peasant's cart, in effect, sacrificing his honor at her behest. Beatrice's expectation that Benedick will obey seems therefore quite reasonable. Benedick's honor is doubly involved, first as Beatrice's lover who has sworn faithful obedience to her, and second as the only capable defender of the honor of his lady's family. To prove himself worthy of her love, he must kill his friend. From such tests of the hero is romance fashioned, from Chrétien's time on. Indeed, *Much Ado* is a cleverer, more effective dramatic handling of the theme of love and honor, the chief *question d'amour* of the traditional romances, than is the earlier *Two Gentlemen*, and as such it is a reaffirmation, not a rejection of the courtly romantic tradition.

What, one wonders, would Shakespeare have replied to the compliment—as it is intended by Price and Stauffer—that he undermined and abandoned the courtly tradition? Surprised amusement, no doubt. But in such supposititious encounters with the spirit of Shakespeare enigma sets in, and we must look elsewhere for indications of what he really thought. Better refer to his audience, for instance, and try to judge what it thought of Shakespeare's use of tradition. Since it returned in large numbers to see the love-game comedy enacted again and again throughout Shakespeare's stay at the Globe, we can well suppose that it felt itself unpurged of addiction to the conventions. The playwright evidently pleased both audience and himself.

We can also compare Greene's work in this vein; quite appropriately, since he complained of Shakespeare's having borrowed his plumes but did not say that Shakespeare dressed himself differently from the established dramatists. No one compliments Greene on having given his age a purge or on having led his characters out from the perfumed, ethical smog of the courtly tradition to the clear, bracing atmosphere of common sense. Greene, although employing the same conventions, the same plumes, so to speak, never arranges them so attractively. He fails to create character from the tensions resulting from the ironic use of the conventions; nor does he hit upon the device (of which Shakespeare might have caught a hint from Lyly's comedies) of strengthening the conventions through exercising them by ironic reversal and humorous mockery. For Greene, they are matters of quite serious wordplay, easily understood dramatic situations, and popular narrative elements. J. C. Collins would have it, though, that "We open Greene's comedies, and we are in the world of Shakespeare . . . we breathe the same atmosphere, we listen to the same language."[9] Thus is the complainant Greene flattered by being told that he is as good as—or almost as good as—the man whose borrowings from his own techniques he had pointed out to the world. Collins's assertions, however, are only very generally true. For specific instance upon instance indicates differences more striking than the similarities.

Margaret, the fair maid of Fressingfield in Greene's *Friar Bacon*, may perhaps dwell in Shakespeare's world. But she would certainly not be among those we would look at twice. She is a creature of milk and water compared with the heroines of even the early comedies: Rosaline and Beatrice and Silvia. So also with Lacy, a poor stick compared with Berowne or Benedick or even Valentine. Why should this be so? Primarily, I suggest, because Greene's characters take the conventions of the love game literally, without either being subject to the ironic commentary of lower-class wooers or themselves experiencing any real conversion from scoffers at love to devotees. The conventions employed by Greene are the same (save for the ironic mockery of the conventions) as those occurring in Shakespeare's romantic comedies. But the difference lies chiefly in what we have already noticed: the deadly earnest with which Greene takes the convention that love ennobles. Fair Margaret will be exalted from the dairy to the court of love, from bourgeois respectability to Earl Lacy's love. She is deemed worthy to grace the courts of love because her virtue will impress even the ladies of Venus's train. Greene is deliberately exploiting a popular theme, one which his auditors would recall with, indeed, some pleasure. But whether this recollection will stir the spirit is doubtful. For the traditional story of beggar maid exalted to princess, with its assumption that goodness of heart can count more than goodness of speech, accent, manners, wit, or dress, is a pleasant one but so fragile, dramatically speaking, that it simply cannot be put to any severe test on stage lest it dissolve into ludicrousness. "A carter," says Turberville in his *Tragicall Tales* (1587), "loves as whotely as a king."[10] Love is a leveler, perhaps, but Shakespeare never subscribes to this democratization of emotions. Hob and Lob, carters in love, may be sentimentally appealing for as long as they inhabit ballad and prose romance. But the headier air and greater demands of the stage prove fatal to them. Shakespeare early learns to avoid littering his stage with such dramatic casualties.

Aside from the comedies where, as even the anticonventionalist Shakespeareans would admit, there is some likelihood of Shakespeare's continuing to use conventional materials and methods because of the nature of the dramatic form, there is the more impressive evidence, so it seems, of Shakespeare's rejection of convention in his tragedies. Shakespeare entitles Romeo to our respectful admiration, it is said, by having him abandon the clichés of the courtly conventions and, forsaking Petrarchism, turn to forthright expressions of honest passion. A well-nigh universal view, this, which scarcely needs documentation. One proponent or accepter of the view might be cited, however, whose judgment more or less sums up all of the others. Boris Pasternak, who translated several of Shakespeare's plays, said of Romeo that he speaks at first unnaturally "in the drawing room manner of his day. But from the moment when he sees Juliet at the ball and stops dead in front of her, not a trace is left of his tuneful mode of expression."[11] The problem here is, once more, characterization. Shakespeare has fools, hypocrites, and the insincere voice conventional beliefs. Hence, it seems to many that conventional lines cannot be spoken with conviction. But Shakespeare knows better. To fashion a tragic hero who can speak the phrases of romantic love, one does not need to change the conventions so much as the tone of voice in which the familiar phrases are spoken. The comments of other characters, moreover, guide the reaction of the audience. The usual opinion that Shakespeare lets us know that Romeo is a changed man by changing his language is flatly contradicted by the amount of the conventional phraseology that persists throughout the play, and Shakespeare further guides our reactions to the early so-called conventional Romeo by Benvolio's and Lady Montague's indulgent comments on his melancholia. We are, therefore, furnished with a ready-made interpretation of his early confession of lovesickness for Rosaline:

> When the devout religion of mine eye
> Maintains such falsehood, then turn tears to fires!
> And these, who, often drown'd, could never die,
> Transparent heretics, be burnt for liars!
>   [I.ii.92–95]

A hero of a love-game comedy could hardly speak more by the book. But Romeo talks pretty much in this fashion throughout the play.

What then really happens when Romeo encounters Juliet? An abandonment of convention? On the contrary, the conventions are suddenly intensified, especially the religion-of-love metaphor which lends itself readily to seriousness and, with complete appropriateness, both to tragedy and comedy. Without Benvolio's having told us that Romeo's early use of the metaphor ("transparent heretics," "religion of mine eye") was inexperienced posing, could we tell that there is a change when Romeo at the Capulet's ball speaks in the same metaphor, addressing Juliet as "dear saint," and referring to kisses as prayers? For there is certainly no rejection of the convention here, no sudden forthrightness resulting from his being freed from the old idolatry. It is, on the contrary, a reaffirmation of the familiar modes of belief of the old religion by a youth expert in the beauteous eloquence of the old faith. This is what is moving. Moreover, the "fair saint" of Romeo's idolatry is visible, young, fresh, and fair and not the Rosaline who, to judge from Mercutio's comments (which are again Shakespeare's hints to us how to interpret the early Romeo) is a bit too marbly frigid and black-browed to adorn a shrine of the goddess of love.

Similarly, the balcony scene is replete with conventional terms that define the traditional relationships of lady and servant in the old religious and feudal metaphors: "It is my lady," "fair saint," "the god of my idolatry." A brief wooing, to be sure, but convincing precisely because, through indicating the whole weight and force of convention, it conveys far more of passion and emotional commitment than would iterations of ingenious and new-found metaphysical images of love. Romeo's sincere belief in the old faith stimulates and involves the audience's old emotional habits; it does not inveigle the auditor's surprised wonder at ingenious attempts to plumb the depths of human passion.

Romeo and Juliet, despite Shakespeare's increasing skill in employing love conventions in compressed form to tell his story and define character, still lacks the perfect joining of the conventions of different genres that marks Shakespeare's great plays. The courtly conventions are excellently used; those of revenge tragedy not so well. The different sets of conventions do not cooperate but stand in contention. This is a problem Shakespeare will solve later in the great tragedies and in the late romances. But *Romeo and Juliet,* his first attempt at romantic tragedy, is marred by a collision of ideas arising from inadequate presentation of the revenge-play conventions. Thus, Romeo is a man of honor with revenge as his duty; he is also conventional lover, ready to obey Juliet's every command. The motives appropriate to these separate characters, however, are not clearly assimilated into one coherent characterization in which they would inspire a struggle of sufficient dimension to make of Romeo a tragic hero.

Romeo's lessoning in the school of love is superbly done. As a demonstration of the art of wooing there can be none better. But the following scenes fail somehow to increase Romeo's ethical stature. He remains immature, pathetic, not tragic. For Shakespeare does not clarify the matter of choice that involves the hero's rejection of his primary loyalty to his mistress where a tragic flaw might become the evident cause of the ensuing disaster. Consequently, the harmony of the play suffers, leading writers to wonder if the unfortunate intrusion of chance in the miscarrying of Friar Laurence's letter is the only real cause of tragedy. Actually, the cause of the disaster should be Romeo's disobedience to the code of love—a point never made quite clear in the play. Furthermore, a too great involvement of the code of love in alien matters such as feuds and family loyalties makes of Juliet a less than independent mistress of her own fate, let alone Romeo's. Shakespeare seems to have neglected this detail when he endowed Juliet with the characteristics of the romantic heroine and then deprived her of freedom to command. Again, pathos rather than tragedy results. For such power does the convention grant the lady that she should have command over her lover's every moral choice. For a moment only we see this when Juliet bids Romeo linger on the morning of his banishment, and he replies:

> Let me be ta'en, let me be put to death.
> I am content, so thou wilt have it so.
>
> [III.v.17–18]

Without the convention in mind, we might think that Romeo is merely teasing Juliet. Indeed, the scene is often played in this key, with a startled Juliet hastily bundling Romeo out into the morn. Actually, Romeo should be, according to the code known to Shakespeare's audience, completely at her command, his life at her disposal. But the relationship has been tainted by Romeo's earlier yielding to the demands of the code of revenge; and his killing of Tybalt is an episode so startling and violent that the attempt to get the love conventions back in control of the play by asserting their equality with the motivations and characterizations of the revenge-play conventions never succeeds.

Romeo, behaving correctly while he endures the taunts of the jeering Tybalt, is undergoing the trial, like Chrétien's knights, of bearing ignominy and loss of honor for the sake of the lady. The trouble is that in a proper romance the hero would be clearly undergoing the test so as to stand well in his lady's graces. But *Romeo and Juliet* fails to place Romeo sufficiently under this command, and he seems, when being jeered at by Tyablt, merely gentle instead of exercising a commanded restraint. The play is like *Troilus and Cressida* in this respect, when Achilles' reluctance to fight is offhandedly, hence inadequately, motivated by his vow to the Trojan princess Polyxena.

Actually, Romeo would have been true to the courtly code if he had endured for his lady's sake even the death of his friend. It is not at the Capulet's ball, or beneath Juliet's balcony, that he breaks with the courtly code, but when he sets off in pursuit of Tybalt:

> O sweet Juliet,
> Thy beauty hath made me effeminate,
> And in my temper soft'ned valor's steel.
> [III.i.118-20]

But our modern interpretation praises Romeo for his slaying of Tybalt as well as for what it fancies his turning away from courtly conventions. One thing is clear: modern minds have a way of simplifying *Romeo and Juliet* by failing to see how many dilemmas it contains. For to put revenge and honor above love is to betray the code of love, and thus cause the ensuing disaster. This is what, I believe, Shakespeare set out to tell. But he let the conventions of the revenge drama become so explosively predominant in this one scene that neither set of conventions, revenge or love, affords a proper resolution to the play. Hence the arbitrary pronouncement by Prince Escalus at the end of the play sounds suspiciously like a passage hastily drawn from the convention of edification so as to furnish the spectators with a sixpence or so of morality on which to meditate on their homeward way. As for us moderns, the best we can make of Romeo's fatal choice of honor over love is a bad critical bargain: the "star-crossed lovers" notion of fate operating through chance.

The brilliancies as well as the inadequacies of *Romeo and Juliet* spring in large part from Shakespeare's filling in the pattern and expanding the plot and characterizations of the source story with aspects of courtly conventions and revenge-play conventions. A masterpiece by any other hand, it remains, in the Shakespeare canon, merely one of the better plays of his apprentice period. *The Merchant of Venice* also suffers from the same imperfect juncture of conventions. The play's two stories, each drawn from a different tradition, clash rather than cooperate. They do not, as in the later tragedies, *Lear*, for instance, reinforce each other by ironic contrasts and similarities.

The Merchant of Venice attempts to fit several stories, as disparate as could be found, into a single play. If this could be successfully managed, all will cooperate to generate tension sufficient to unite elements as unlikely of assimilation as the Jew plot and casket plot. More discord than unity, however, results from the clash between a group of characters drawn from romance and one figure drawn from the revenge play. The episodes of the main plot and their theme are all romantic; the subplot is an obvious exploitation of a figure that begins as comic derivative from the Vice and ends as would-be revenger, a crushed but unrepentant villain, whose malevolence still threatens the harmony decreed by the conventions of romance.

The Merchant of Venice contains some hints as to how and why Shakespeare altered source stories. Some have blanketed all such changes under the easy explanation that it was his genius, working with extraordinary insights into human nature. This, however, is an unsatisfactory explanation, for it leaves more unsaid than it elucidates. How, after all, does dramatic genius get down to cases? Must it wait until, prodded into action by happy but unwitting inspiration, it engages in the creative process hardly aware of what it is doing? Or

does it have habits of its own plus tricks of its own devising of
which it is calculatingly aware? Probably the latter, for some
pattern or habit of workmanship suggests itself in the changes
Shakespeare made while weaving together elements from
three sources. *Il Pecorone*, *Gesta Romanorum*, and Marlowe's *Jew of Malta* (or, perhaps, an older play mentioned by
Gosson in his *School of Abuse*).

In the source story, *Il Pecorone*, the character of Portia,
the Lady of Belmont, is greedy, vain, powerful, malevolent,
and suddenly lascivious, winning ducats from her young suitors by wagering that they cannot possess her, though sharing
her bed, but first drugging their wine at dinner. Warned by a
friendly serving maid, one hardy youth avoids the drugged
wine, wins the third night's wager, and pleases the lady so well
in bed that she endows him with all of her wealth. A pretty
sort of story, one must say, to put on the stage before the good
people of London. Therefore, say some critics, Shakespeare
refurbished it, morally speaking, by adding the casket plot, a
rather well-known little story that makes a pleasing dumb-
show spectacle to delight the patrons and excuse the Lady of
Belmont from exercising her dubious appetites.

Shakespeare, in this view, is a moralist catering to the
sensibilities of his audience. This is in a way true, for unlike
Ford or Webster, Shakespeare perpetrates no unpleasant surprises about sexual depravity. But to ascribe the changes in
plot to a supposed instinct for bourgeois morality on Shakespeare's part does not give much insight into Portia's character,
and, of course, leaves wholly unexamined the Shylock plot,
making of it a bit of dramatic quixoticism, as if Shakespeare
were trying to see how many stories it is possible to combine
into one play. To be sure, this may be at least part of Shakespeare's motivation. But we are yet left to find the more significant guide or principle of dramaturgy that Shakespeare habitually follows in adapting sources. That guiding principle is, as
merely tracking down sources can hardly show us, a loyalty to
the tradition that governs the characterizations and situations
of all such stories. The Lady of Belmont becomes the same sort
of person as Rosalind of *Love's Labour's Lost* and Julia of *Two*

Gentlemen; and as Beatrice, Rosalind, and Viola are to be. To her endowment with the conventional attributes of the *midons* of old romance is added the wit of Renaissance wordplay involving the metaphors of the love-game comedy. Shakespeare sharpens all of these in dramatic conflict not only with the situations of the complicating subplots but with the conventions of revenge stories. In this play, however, he permits this last conflict to go beyond the possibilities of final and dramatically sound resolution.

As is proper in romance, the lady becomes the object of pilgrimage, and the story shapes itself according to the metaphor of the religion of love. Antonio asks Bassanio, for instance,

> Well, tell me now, what lady is the same
> To whom you swore a secret pilgrimage,
> That you today promis'd to tell me of?
> [I.i.119–21]

The secrecy enjoined by the code, the pilgrimage reminiscent of the journeys of lovers in old romances and allegories—it could hardly be more closely adapted.

The Lady of Belmont, object of Bassanio's love pilgrimage, is, like the heroine of romance, at last the commander of her lover's weal and not, as in the source story, a Circe betrayed by her own lust. At first she is threatened by the forbidding strictures of her father's will that apparently deny her the freedom, conventionally accorded heroines of courtly romance, to choose her lover. After the perils of having to accept an unwelcome suitor have passed, however, her wit enables her to evade the intolerable conditions of her father's will by ever-so-delicately indicating which casket is the proper choice for the man to whom she intends to grant her favor.

Ingeniously contrived as these situations are, Shakespeare seems to take even more delight in the ironies resulting from the interplay of the trial setting and the court-of-love conventions. Portia becomes, in disguise, not only a justiciar of Venice but thereafter a judge in a most traditional *débat d'amour. The* matter debated in the posttrial scene is one of the oldest and most often posed questions: is love stronger than friendship? When Bassanio at Antonio's urging yields to the claim of friendship and gives the ring to "the learned judge," Portia, he in effect breaks love's vows, his only defense being that honor bade him give away his lady's ring. It is a case of honor versus love in which both the betrayed lady and the judge are one, a proper position of strength, one might add, and in terms of the convention the right one for her. The only way out for a lover thus entrapped is to throw himself on the mercy of the court. Of course, as Bassanio does this he remembers, as we should, Portia's eloquent urgings of mercy in the trial scene. Forgiveness of penitent lovers is, after all, a proper ending for romantic comedy.

Shakespeare's audience must have noted many other familiar conventions. Indeed, the play is remarkably full of odds and ends thrown in for good measure. In Gobbo, for example, the Vice shows up briefly, betraying his provenance in his opening speech as he rehearses a little morality concerning, if we may invent a title, the contest of Conscience and Diabolus for the soul of Gobbo. But Gobbo is morally remade early in the play by going from wicked master to good and remaining there in the simpler role of licensed jester.[12]

Romance suffers a dearth of genuine villains to stir up real trouble. The most the courtly tradition can do, for example, is to provide a scoffer at love who, after having perpetrated some verbal mischief, is converted into penitent lover. In order to construct a drama, however, there is needed some way of arousing genuine apprehension of serious harm to hero and heroine. To effect this, a stereotype villain is conveniently at hand in the figure of the scheming Vice and his progeny, the revenge-play Machiavellian, who pursues mischief sometimes for revenge, and sometimes for the mere fun of stirring up trouble. In order to introduce this kind of character into the play's structure, the curious anomaly of the romantic pilgrimage financed as a risk venture of Antonio's capital is let stand, for it explains the presence of Shylock the moneylender, who will take up the role of villain.

Shakespeare's critics, however, seem to want to ignore the

conventional aspects of Shylock's role. They try to account for his disrupting influence by saying that he talks too much, that he is too eloquent, that he is too real a character for such a play, and so on. Actually, Shakespeare does not create a startlingly new, hence dramatically uncontrollable figure; he combines several stock types. Shylock is given the usual traits of the Jew of legend, sorting well enough with the Elizabethans' crude notion of racial psychology. But, more important for the action of the play, Shylock is, early in the play, remarkably like the Vice who pretends to be counselor and friend to all. Endow him with what Shakespeare's contemporaries believed to be Jewish malevolence and spite, and he seems to be more than a stock character. For he exhibits motivations appropriate to disparate stereotypes, thus impressing us as a complex figure subject to all degrees of psychological and sociological analysis. He agrees to lend money without interest, to sign a merry bond. Here is the ingratiating, scheming Vice. Whichever way things turn out, he profits. If the bond is not forfeit, he will have pleased his hypocrisy; if it is forfeit, he will have a way of stirring up some trouble for its own sake. Given a more specific motive for revenge, however, the character seems to develop. He takes villainy more seriously, so to speak, and becomes in effect the revenge-play villain. If we view Shylock as a composite, we can see better why audiences and critics are troubled by him. He is a threat not simply to the other characters but to the integrity of the play itself.

The conventional villain of a revenge play, with additional extraordinary identification as the Jew, can do nothing but undermine the tradition that governs the other parts of the play. Again, the romance and revenge-play conventions, having been thus set in opposition, cannot be brought into any proper or final relationship—either by having the revenge-play conventions win out in a tragic ending, or by having the conventions of the love game triumph, which, of course, would give us comedy. The difficulty is that Shylock cannot be made a repentant convert to the role of kind father to Jessica—which would involve him ludicrously in condoning the religion-of-love tradition—nor can he be revengefully victorious, his identification being too grossly and outspokenly definite for him to practice the subtle hypocrisy of Iago.

The play has to be forced to some kind of closure, however, and for this Shakespeare has recourse to the convention that, both dramatically and morally, has always proved serviceable to him, the religion-of-love metaphor. We can see him moving the pieces into position for the final scene, all the more obviously because his efforts to counter the effect of the trial scene that ends with the unlovely picture of Shylock's shuffling malevolence and hate as he departs must by antipathy be more conspicuous. The obvious and expected contrary to Shylock's hate is Jessica's love. The obvious converse of the revenge-play conventions is the religion of love. Why, we wonder, does this neat plan not work better? Like other commentators on the play, I have to blame Shylock, but not simply because he is too talkative, making speeches that persuade us of the cruel injustice of the judgment against him. I find fault with him becasue he is compounded of so many revenge-play conventions that he saps the strength of the play's romance conventions and prevents the play from attaining true dramatic unity. The two plots from which the play is fashioned remain in opposition.

This estrangement affects other characters, Jessica, for example: she is a convert to Christianity and also to the religion of love. An interesting doubling of meaning to be sure, but a bit too strong to usher in the dramatic tranquillity which might follow if she were, more conventionally, merely a convert to the religion of love and through this new faith freed from parental tyranny. Double the vigor of her revolt, however, and the result is a figure not quite adaptable to the role of custodian of Belmont. For a time, nevertheless, the metaphors of the religion of love provide a mood of tranquillity and harmony as Lorenzo and Jessica recite antiphonally the litany of the martyrs of love with its melancholy accounts of those who died for love so that present lovers may be secure in their faith that love endures. It is indeed a pleasant preparation for the return

of the other lovers to Belmont. Would they were not returning
from the law courts of Venice and their triumph over an enemy whose hatred, although checked, lives as strong as ever.

Moral edification in the form of happy endings of romance or punishments of villains in tragedy is reassuringly
palatable and, as the apprentice Shakespeare knew, easily
vendible. It would, of course, enhance the drawing power of
the history play, for the Elizabethan judicious spectator expected to find instructiveness made explicit in the form of the
received truisms of historical and political theory voiced by
official spokesmen, commentators, and kings, and the like. And
he might even welcome reminiscences of an older dramatic
fashion that presented the good and evil in men's affairs acted
out by personified abstractions.

References to conventional political doctrines so permeate
Shakespeare's histories that the plays constitute an elucidation
of Renaissance theory. Explications of God's will as chief
guide for the ordered commonwealth fall easily from the lips
of Richmond before Bosworth; and Prince John at the end of
2 *Henry IV* orates similarly to an appreciative audience. Such
expected lessons for the auditory must always have been occasions of solemnity. Thus with the opening scene of *Henry V,*
which contains Canterbury's disquisition on the commonwealth of bees and his immediate application of the lesson to
the troubled state of Henry's realm. We may be sure that
Shakespeare's audience made sense of the speech and re-
spected the good prelate for his wisdom. Observe, however,
how embarrassed modern producers are with the scene, making the archbishop the epitome of pomposity, and enlivening
matters, as in the Olivier film, with cascades of parchments
dropped by the fumbling Exeter—all of this to amuse the
groundlings, for the modern producer evidently believes that
Shakespeare's audience had to be tricked into listening to a
play by being treated first to a guffaw.

Statements of policy, however, do not by themselves create character. But when Shakespeare attributes such notions
to less exalted persons than the rulers and leaders of men, subtleties of characterization and of theme are suggested. Thus

with the metaphor of the unweeded garden, as potent a metaphor for the history play as the religion of love is for romantic comedy. The gardener in *Richard II* guides our judgment of the king, justly pictured as a slovenly caretaker of the fair garden entrusted to him by God. So it would remain—a graceful phrasing of a political cliché—save that the queen overhears. Her reaction, all the more passionate because she knows the reproach is sound, depicts for us a woman troubled alike by pity for Richard and by awareness of his failings. So also with the audience: we must pity Richard, yet condemn him.

The theme of the gardener's discourse is echoed in another set speech toward the end of the play when Richard in prison recalls earlier and happier times. It is as if he were responding to the gardener's speech and, as he peoples his imaginary commonwealth, were making amends, however ineffectual. He puts into his ideal state the proper arrangement of orders and degrees of society, "silly beggars as well as the better sort," and, we note, incorporates also the principle of unrest that in history is at once society's vitality and its disease. What a wise king he is, now at rest in meditation after having himself caused the infection of unrest that enfeebled his realm.

By the time he writes *Richard II* and *Henry IV*, Shakespeare has come a long way in his apprenticeship from the artificialities of the *Henry VI* plays in which set pieces edify about the wounds of civil war. True, the gardener's speech and Richard's last speech are set, long, and formal; but Shakespeare elicits theme and character from them. In later plays, however, characterization appears even in the comments that follow a seemingly chance reference to the correspondence of nature and men's affairs. Prince Hal, before the battle of Shrewsbury, remarks on the gloom overhanging the field. King Henry, instead of accepting the platitude of nature's mood reflecting the affairs of men, retorts rather waspishly and with Machiavellian astuteness:

> Then with the losers let it sympathize,
> For nothing can seem foul to those that win.
> [*Henry IV, Part I*, V.i.7–8]

Such twisting of the conventional reference is in keeping with Henry's later confession of devious purposes and points in its unobtrusive way to the troubled heart of the matter: Henry's dubious seizure of the crown may be akin to the storms and tumults that rend nature's peace, yet so puzzlingly seem an ineluctable consequence of the working of the forces of nature itself. Again by the anagogical inference so dear to the medieval mind, which bequeathed the same habit to the Renaissance, such tumults betoken the inevitability of recurrent disorder in men's historical experience.

Henry is master of all moods, for if Shakespeare gives him the ability to twist convention so as to evade the true "lesson" of the convention, that is, tempests are foul to all men not only to losers, he also endows Henry with the ability to impress the audience as well as other characters in the play with his phrasings of the metaphors involving nature, order, and the state. Thus, when speaking to rebels, his mouth is worked by ancient memories as he addresses a homily to Worcester, counseling him on a subject's proper duty to adjure rebellion

> And move in that obedient orb again
> Where you did give a fair and natural light;
> And be no more an exhal'd meteor,
> A prodigy of fear, and a portent
> Of broached mischief to the unborn times.
> [*Henry IV, Part I*, V.i.17–21]

Awkwardly obtrusive as some of the edificatory speeches are, Shakespeare uses them as well in these early plays as any other playwright of the time. What he learns, and his fellow playwrights do not, is the technique of combining the motives of individual characters, as often revealed in their ironic, hypocritical use of the familiar metaphor or in their seriously intended use of the known figures of speech, with the grander projection of the metaphor onto a level of reference which affords, on the one hand, the vista of history found so stimulatingly edifying by the Elizabethans and, on the other, a universal pattern, tragic in essence, of the never-ceasing ebb and flow of order and disorder, the everlasting contention between

God's order and man's refractory nature. This is the same over-arching scheme that broods over the great tragedies.

History-play characters whose speeches are replete with metaphors of order and disorder tend to resemble personifications—more vividly garbed in particular manners and speech than the personifications of the Morality, but recognizable descendants, in lineament and habits of speech, of figures like *Mundus, Caro,* and *Diabolus.* It used to be said, however, that Shakespeare and his generation of dramatists very wisely banished personified abstractions from the stage and let humanity appear in its proper guise and speech. J. W. Cunliffe, for instance, found so poor a play as Richard Edwards's *Damon and Pythias* praiseworthy because it omitted the abstractions that had earlier cluttered the stage.[13] Strange that the absence of abstractions should have been thus hailed, for actually they stubbornly continued to tread the boards, and E. K. Chambers finds some eighteen Elizabethan plays that listed personified abstractions as characters.[14] But the abstractions had subtler ways of enduring than brashly intruding as completely visible personifications upon the stage of the 1590s, and of late their sly presence has been increasingly noted even in Shakespeare's plays, in Falstaff's being termed "Grey Iniquity" by Prince Hal,[15] for example, or even in the tragedies where reminiscences of the Vice, a supercompound of abstractions, prompt Hamlet's antic disposition.

Such discoveries, however, should not surprise. Shakespeare, after all, was astute enough to recognize the value of old dramatic usages, especially when played off against new ones. The history play with its habitual reference to world schemes cannot fail to welcome characters that direct attention, and therefore a measure of understanding, to articles of generally accepted wisdom. Here again, as with the courtly conventions, Shakespeare begins with an obvious and fully explicated convention. Falconbridge, for example, in *King John* is a fully elaborated character, who insists upon telling us his provenance in the Vice Commodity. At first he is the jesting Vice, furnisher of comic relief, endowed with license of ubiquity and free comment. The history play cannot very well exist without this kind of character, for by his timely appearances to comment on the actions of the shakers and movers, he brings continuity to the successive political arrangements and derangements of which the play is constituted. He is, in effect, a structural feature without which it would be well-nigh impossible to fashion a drama from chronicle material.

Falconbridge, however, is actually two stereotypes, and in Act IV changes from Vice to honest counselor of the sovereign. Beginning as a fully drawn and simply depicted Vice with his unsubtle identification of himself as "tickling Commodity, that smooth-fac'd gentleman," busy in the affairs of kings and princes, he claims to be about to play Commodity's role with a difference. He will, he says, retain his sense of humor in a mad world and learn deceit in order to avoid being deceived. But suddenly he drops the role of mad wag to become an official voice of England's policy, who discovers in his shocked dismay at young Arthur's death his own natural probity. Thus he is metamorphosed rather than developed into the figure of the honest counselor, another stock character from the older dramas where kings were surrounded by both good and wicked advisers and deprived of initiative of their own.

This abrupt change of character is a flaw in the play, of course, indicative of the playwright's inadequate structuring of his play. He could have built more securely with a stereotype figure presented with some judiciously suggested variations from a familiar pattern. Actually, Shakespeare begins his characterization of Falconbridge in this way, effectively tempering the character's stereotype qualities with the boasts of being able to play his role with a difference. But he lets this side of the character fall silent and has him speak thereafter with the voice of an altogether different stereotype. How different this is from Shakespeare's skillful construction of the later history plays around the character of Falstaff, who like Falconbridge bears the identifying marks of the Vice, but unlike Falconbridge consistently develops and exploits the Vice characteristics.

The orderly world of the romance was dependent upon such conventions as the court of love, the school of love, and the commandments of love. All of these conventions lent themselves so admirably to drama that success awaited the dramatist who employed them well; and if, like Shakespeare, he used them with irony and deception and final affirmation, his success was guaranteed in his own time and after. Why not, then, construct history plays along the same model and out of counterpart conventions? A court of love is an appropriate form for the romance; the king's court is obviously suitable for history. If the school of love is a natural form for romantic narrative, perhaps the schooling of the prince might be seemly for history. If the parody of the court of love is proper for the low characters of romance, a mock court or a parody of the king's court might be seemly for historical drama. Thus the *Henry IV* plays and *Henry V* employ the structure but not the content (until the wooing scene in *Henry V*) of the romantic comedy: the schooling of the prince takes place, in part, in the parody of the king's court, that is, in Falstaff's court of misrule. Falstaff, most appropriately, is inspirer of both the parody of the school of the prince and of the royal court. In the first role, he exercises considerable ingenuity in tampering with familiar conventions so as to insinuate himself into our sophisticated toleration. Whereas, like the wicked counselor of youth, he should be the acknowledged corrupter, he tries to appropriate our approval to himself. (Hal is, after all, humorously tolerant of him; why then should not we allow the same scope to the fat knight?) He does this by outrageously attempting to turn the conventional relationship upside down, improvising the role of the corrupter corrupted when he allows the prince to persuade him to engage in the expedition to Gadshill. "Before I knew thee, Hal, I knew nothing; and now am I, if a man should speak truly, little better than one of the wicked" (I.ii.103–6).

Falstaff, when we observe him closely, behaves like a king in his own right. He rules a court of his own and has dealings with an emissary from the head of another state, the lord chief justice. Consider also his group of followers, all devotees of misrule (or better yet, no rule), all eagerly awaiting the time when, they hope, their master Falstaff shall have reduced England to his governance. Falstaff also makes alliances and serves King Henry against the common enemies, Percy and Northumberland. Actually, he serves himself in this, for his existence depends upon his battening upon an orderly society. If Percy triumphs, farewell the ordered state and the days of peaceful roistering and parasitism and assured victims. How nicely the convention is made to fit the actuality—or would it be more proper to call the convention a projection of actuality? In the world of fact, unless history and sociology deceive us, the hypocrite, racketeer, and sponger can exist only when a society sets some norm by which their behavior can be judged. As soon as such an order is established, they appear as if symbiotically related. In a pure anarchy they could not exist, for there is no power or ruler for them to protest against while they pluck the victims made fat by the days of ordered plenty. So also in the drama. A system, an orderly relationship, established or implied, serves as object of the subversion intended by clown, jester, or mocking commentator. No wonder, then, that Falstaff must be regarded as indispensable, for he contributes to the politically instructive quality of the play in a more telling way than even Percy and his rebellion. For Falstaff with his mockery court of misrule tests more subtly the strength of the real court than ever Percy could. The king's court, symbol of conventional political doctrine, survives this test intact, a test which is analogous (in the structure as well as theme of the play) to the probation of the court of love and its conventions by the clowns of the romantic comedies. The revolt of the Percies, however, represents the force of disorder at work in a more familiar pattern, and Shakespeare writes this part of his drama in straightforward manner, giving us Percy, rebellion and disorder, against Hal, order and rule.

Without Falstaff, the *Henry IV* plays might be, indeed, a superior chronicle account colored with meditations upon honor and expressing the nice balance of prudence, strength, and capacity for deception required to rule successfully. But Shakespeare was not content with this much excellence; with

Falstaff's assistance he makes of the play a vehicle of delight and instruction. Falstaff must at last, however, become expendable in terms of the political wisdom the play intends to impart. From this demand of the theme of the play arises the predicament in which audiences and commentators find themselves when considering the fortunes of Falstaff.

The fortunes of Falstaff are, in sum, these: a promising future indeed he has for a while when enthroned at the Boar's Head Tavern he plays the mock king. But he is not allowed to play out the play. Prince Hal departs abruptly, leaving Falstaff to cry, "Play out the play—I have much to say in behalf of that Falstaff." Actually, there is nothing more to say in his behalf. The defense is in; his role defined; and the limitations upon that role foretold, for Hal in concluding the parody announces his resolve to banish plump Jack. Falstaff's plea for more time for his defense is only his bravado—and Shakespeare's too.

It is pleasant to catch a dramatist claiming to be able to develop some conventional character or situation beyond what could by any rule of dramatic feasibility be successfully done. No more could be said in Falstaff's behalf, nor could his role in the play be any more enlarged. Indeed, Shakespeare verges close on disaster as far as the *Henry IV* plays are concerned, not because Elizabethan audiences would resent Hal's banishing Falstaff, for the issues would be understood aright and praise rather than blame would be accorded the new king for his rejection of "grey iniquity." Rather, the balance of the play is called into question (this is the same flaw that mars *The Merchant of Venice*) if the stereotype were allowed to seize too much of the play as his domain. To put it another way, Falstaff's role grows to the point where it is in danger of offering conflict rather than the tension arising from the way in which subsidiary characters in the episodic and well-peopled Elizabethan stage play practice their mockery and ironic imitation of the principal, and edificatory, themes. Shakespeare evidently decided to confine such characters (Parolles, Dogberry, Autolycus) more strictly to their conventional roles or to push the development of the stock character to the point where he becomes a full-fledged antagonist (Iago or Edmund or Iachimo). At any rate, dramatic aberrations like Shylock will not again trouble Shakespeare (save in *Troilus and Cressida*). Falstaff's banishment in a way is Shakespeare's victory over them.

The plumes which Greene accused Shakespeare of purloining were numerous indeed. But there were some which Shakespeare did not borrow. Among this neglected plumage were some tricks of which Greene was himself extremely fond, especially the extravagant, fanciful romanticization of history. Greene, no respecter of persons, made of the great ones of history a group of heroes of romantic encounters. We have noted his *Ciceronis Amor* in which the glamour of the great name is intended to dignify the clichés of romance. Take also *James IV* in which there is attempted as outlandish a combination of romance and history as we are likely to find in any present-day historical novel or motion picture. Why, one wonders, did not Shakespeare also take this seemingly easy road to popularity? A sterner aesthetic conscience, of course, prevented his becoming a peddler of banalities—but that alone would not explain Shakespeare's success and Greene's failure on the stage. There must be something that the audience contributed—that is, a certain amount of discrimination that in the long run disliked Greene's abusing its willing suspension of disbelief.

Having said this, however, one must pause to consider Shakespeare's treatment of Richard III. Surely the courting of Lady Anne is a gross importation of fictional romance into history, as bad as anything of which Greene is guilty. There is no warrant in history for such a scene any more than there is for James IV's attempting the virtue of Ida, chaste daughter of the Countess of Arran. James's attempt is intended to be outrageous and shocking, but sentimentality intrudes, and in Greene's play pallid virtue triumphs, whereas in *Richard III* the pallor of moral sickness taints the lady's cheek.

Shakespeare is not, however, trying to emulate Greene, or any one of his contemporaries. He is experimenting with combinations of conventional plot situations and characterizations. He seems automatically or instinctively to have rejected those that are bound to fail—like the sentimentalization of chronicle accounts—and further toughened and hardened those which had elements of toughness in them already. This is what goes on in *Richard III*. The sources offer little to go on as far as Richard's wooing of Lady Anne is concerned, for they merely hint darkly that Richard's marrying his victim's widow was somehow connected with his plans for acquiring property and a tenuous connection with Lancastrian interests. The lady's feelings were not important—she is an object, not a person. Shakespeare, however, has at hand the example of the romance's mocker at love and the Marlovian Machiavellian whose tricks hark back to the Vice's exploits. He also has in mind, and has characterized her well in other plays, the heroine of courtly romance who has absolute command over her lover's fate, but who is under the certain obligation of yielding to her lover once she is satisfied of his good faith, the soundness of his protestations of fidelity, and the genuineness of his submission to her will. How neatly all of these are exploited in the scene of Richard's encounter with Anne—the whole tradition compressed into a few lines; the whole course of wooing, with the lessons of the school of love rehearsed. All the while there is the accompanying undercurrent of mockery of the conventions and their hypocritical exploitation by one skilled in confounding others by appealing to their loyalty to ideals.

The explanation that Lady Anne, like actual women of medieval times, is merely a pawn of feudal interests for whom women were convenient means of acquiring rights of inheritance and holding of fiefs or preventing disseisin will not suffice. True, for actual women of the fifteenth century the protection of men was their only way of surviving; therefore, Anne is doubly susceptible to Richard's suit, for without his protection her prospects, as she follows the corpse of her father-in-law, the king, to makeshift burial, seem dubious indeed. This matter-of-fact explanation, however, has no pertinence to drama. It belongs in the history books, not on the stage. For Shakespeare never intimates any other motive for Lady Anne than that provided by the courtly tradition. She is not timorous or apprehensive about the future. Nor does she seem impressed by Richard's high rank and glittering prospects—all of which may have been in the mind of the histori-

cal Lady Anne. What does overcome her hatred and disdain
is the proof Richard offers her of his love. He gives his life into
her hands—the words of the old convention acted out literally
as he bares his breast to the sword he vows to use at her
command.

It is always shocking to see familiar conventional statements, worn smooth with time, taken literally. Obviously both
Richard and Shakespeare know this: Richard senses that Anne
will be convinced; Shakespeare knows that the audience, however incredulous at first, will approve of the outcome as sound
and subtle characterization. So subtle indeed is the characterization that some suspicion attaches to Lady Anne, as if she
were abnormally fascinated by Richard and perversely desirous of mating with deformed evil. Here again, character is
generated from the opposition of conventions, each contribut-
ing the nuances in which the truth of human nature is revealed. To Lady Anne there is no proof to the contrary concerning Richard's statements that he slew her husband for love
of her, risking mortal dangers in war to prove himself worthy
of her. But we, of course, know him for Machiavel. Put the devout language of the old tradition into the mouth of a malevolent but humorous stereotype Machiavellian, have him address
a fair lady knowledgeable only in the language of the feudal
and religious metaphors of love which have customarily been
accepted by the audience as morally sound, and the same surprises of psychology and morality result as arise from the admixture of conventions, later on, in *Hamlet*.

Richard III is, indeed, surprisingly full of romantic conventions. We should expect, for example, in so royally entitled
a drama, the usual opening of a history play: a political or
warlike declaration. Instead, Richard appears not as the expected figure of the history play concerned with war or proph-
ecies of disaster, but as the conventional mocker of love, jeering at the courtly lover who

> Capers nimbly in a lady's chamber
> To the lascivious pleasing of a lute.
>   [I.i.12–13]

When he meets Lady Anne, the metaphors of the religion of love are everywhere apparent. Richard, having hypocritically changed roles from mocker of love to conventional lover, speaks like a devil (Lady Anne's apt term for him on first addressing him), who can of course quote the scriptures of love as well as of true religion. Richard has the code of the lover by heart, addressing Anne as an "angry angel," object of his adoration. After his success, he lapses into his former role, exulting in his triumph:

> Was ever woman in this humor woo'd?
> Was ever woman in this humor won?
>> [I.ii.227–28]

The answer to Richard's questions must be yes, of course. The "humor" must be the familiar convention or the scene would fail. But to see the "humor" employed by a character whom we have been taught to loathe is novel and astonishing.

If those who like to find Shakespeare busy at undermining courtly traditions wanted to make a more persuasive case, they might do better by citing this scene than the early romantic comedies. For if the conventions are so obviously susceptible to manipulation and distortion (and Richard shows that this can easily be done), they should be abjured as frail reeds inadequate to support any sound morality. This would be more ethically cogent than saying that since Shakespeare in his comedies sports with the conventions, they are ridiculous and must be abandoned.

Shakespeare's virtuosity in this scene has seldom if ever been equaled. His imitators, especially among the Jacobeans, attempted to create the same combination of shock, astonishment, and psychological surprise by outraging some conventional moral tenet. Beaumont and Fletcher, for example, in *The Maid's Tragedy* present Evadne as a lady skilled in the wordplay of courtly love but at heart a disbeliever. A hardened case, if there ever was one. When Amyntor, beside himself with delight at her having consented to wed him, behaves like a courtly lover in the bedchamber, choosing to believe that her refusal to yield to him is motivated by her modest regard for her precious chastity (the lady of romance must by custom be reluctant to be won), Evadne uses the language of *fin amour* first to assert her dominance over him as agent of her revenge upon the king:

> Now I shall try thy truth; if thou dost love me
> Thou weigh'st not anything compar'd with me;
> Life, Honor, Joys Eternal, all Delights
> This world can yield, or hopeful people feign,
> Or in the life to come, are light as Air
> To the true lover when his lady frowns,
> And bids him do thus: wilt thou kill this man?
>
> [II.i 174–80]

She sounds for all the world like Beatrice demanding that Benedick kill Claudio. She has the vocabulary, however, but not the faith, and turns Amyntor's jealous hate rather than his obedient service to her command against her enemy. In other words, she does not trust the motivations of the old beliefs, but goes on to disillusion Amyntor most cruelly with her reply to his wistful inquiry about her purity: "A maidenhead, Amyntor, at my years?"

One can imagine the audience's derisive snicker at this shattering of poor Amyntor's naïve illusion that the old loyalties of the courtly code were still strongly felt motivations for wellborn and wellbred people. This reaction is quite different from the astonished disgust that greets Richard's successful manipulation of the convention. No one has ever snickered at Richard's triumph. But both scenes deal with the same tradition; both show subverters of the conventions scoring direct hits. The difference in tone between the two scenes is the crucial point. Shakespeare persuades us to affirm the soundness of the ideals embodied in the tradition; the audience judges against Richard and views Anne with a mixture of pity and condemnation. Beaumont and Fletcher, however, try to elicit a feeling of jeering superiority from the audience on witnessing the discomfiture of the naïve traditionalist. Thus the tradition itself is irreparably damaged. The audience is not invited, as in Shakespeare's plays, to support tradition; it is invited to deride, to be more sophisticated than the tradition.

True, Evadne's later sufferings might constitute a kind of atonement. But this cannot compensate for her having made a mockery of the true lover's protestation, for with the loss of dignity Amyntor becomes merely pathetic. Where Shakespeare adds strength to the tradition, Beaumont and Fletcher weaken it.[16] Shakespeare's romantic heroes are, to be sure, sometimes the object of jest: Benedick, for example, and Orlando. But they are not humiliated, and they do not become pathetically hopeless. Throughout Shakespeare's use of the conventions which make up the romantic tradition, the hero's dignity is always either maintained or regained. The true decorum of good drama is thus to uphold dignity of character. When this is lost, greatness disappears. Beaumont and Fletcher, not Shakespeare, by their misuse of conventions "give the age a purge," with the unfortunate result that the romance conventions and the values they symbolize are alike enfeebled.

Shakespeare's secret is in part, at least, a balancing act, in which tradition is challenged, even made sport of for a time, but always restated and approved of at the conclusion of the play. Put more crudely, Amyntor is a fool to be laughingly pitied; Orlando, though foolish at times, is at the end of the play wisely dignified and happy. No one, however, can take the courtly conventions seriously at the end of *The Maid's Tragedy* after Evadne has been so ruthless at their expense.

But, it will be urged, *The Maid's Tragedy* cannot be taken seriously at any point. It is as far removed from actuality as the fictionalized history of Shakespeare's *Richard III*, to say nothing of *Much Ado* or *As You Like It*, and to puzzle over points of moral doctrine and the ethics of the conventions is to reason like philosophers of Laputa. The answer to this objection may be found, as nearly as it can be determined, in the audience's reaction. We dislike, as surely as did Shakespeare's audience, Richard's clever hypocrisy, already clearly defined for us before he encounters Lady Anne. Surely such dislike has ethical as well as psychological validity. Our hatred of Richard and our loyalty to whatever he seeks to undo are for us aspects of reality. We sense these emotions; they are real. But Beaumont and Fletcher end their play with no valid psychological truth at all, hence no valid characterization. Evadne's cruelty, Amyntor's naïvete—neither is more than a clever trick at the expense of the audience's sensibilities. No moral involvement results. Shakespeare's audience was accustomed to taking sides, and so are we. Hence the scene of Richard's wooing of Lady Anne, even in this present antitraditionalist age, fascinates audiences and sets Shakespeareans to psychological analysis of the characters involved. More striking is the envy this scene arouses in modern playwrights, whose skill is all too often closer to that of Beaumont and Fletcher than to Shakespeare's. Even a modern specialist in pathos like the TV playwright Paddy Chayefsky wistfully comments that if he could write as effective a scene as Richard's encounter with Lady Anne, he would feel that he had at last succeeded.[17]

V

The Globe Plays

Stealth and cunning marked the sudden removal of the Chamberlain's men from Holywell to the Bankside in the winter of 1598–99. It was a fortunate move, as it happened; for this company, with the energetic Burbages as entrepreneurs and Shakespeare as the best dramatist of the time, was perfectly equipped to take advantage of the improved estate of the theater. All spirits must have lifted at the sight of the new Globe in 1599, the handsomest theater of the city. This change of locale heralds a change in Shakespeare's art, as if he were abandoning journeyman status to launch into creating one masterpiece after another, failing, as in *Troilus and Cressida*, only when writing for an audience other than that to which the Chamberlain's Men, or as they were termed after 1603, the King's Men, usually catered.

The explanation for this flowering must be that Shakespeare felt at last wholly confident of his skill, hence his ability to hold his audience. It must, moreover, have been much the same audience for which he had written at the Theatre in Holywell. For the removal from Holywell to the Bankside was if anything toward a location more convenient to the city. Near London Bridge and the ferrymen's crafts on the Thames, it had easier access than the crowded, narrow ways toward Shoreditch. Accustomed, then, to the plaudits of this audience and undoubtedly responsive to praise such as Meres's in *Palladis Tamia* of 1598, knowing himself master of his craft, and having hit upon the ways of harmonizing the audience's expectations with his own standards of dramatic craftsmanship,

Shakespeare was ready for his period of mastery. In discussing these plays, one runs the risk, perhaps, of pushing the search for conventions to an extreme and of discerning their presence in places where they are so diminished in importance that they have, in effect, disappeared. I do not believe, however, that Shakespeare's drama ever reaches this point. For despite the increasing complexity of these plays, the conventions continue to be integral parts of their structure. Shakespeare's modesty continues to respect time-honored usages (if they are dramatically effective), but his cunning makes all seem new and hitherto unseen in quite the same light.

If we had playbills for the first two years of operation of the new Globe, however, we would think at first that most of the plays came from the same shop as the plays of the old Theatre. At the head of the roster stand two of the best examples of romantic comedy, as if the new venture had been started with the expectation of a generous financial return for plays guaranteed to please. There is also, however, a play concerning great Rome, with larger tragic scope than the English history plays. *As You Like It, Twelfth Night,* and *Julius Caesar* all bear the mark of an invigorated and refreshed talent, sure of its touch in narrative pattern, deft in characterization, and showing greater skill in verse and dramaturgy. All three plays, however, are based squarely upon familiar conventions. Our task will be first to see how these plays which were, quite probably, Shakespeare's first triumphs at the Globe vary from his apprentice plays in the use of conventions and at the same time continue much of the same usages.

As You Like It, for example, takes us to ground at once familiar and new. The settings in Arden are constituted of familiar raw material and peopled with familiar types. Everything and everyone, however, seem fashioned more clearly and cleverly. Take, for instance, the heralding notes of the expected encounter of young lovers in the familiar school-of-love pattern, a convention which dominates the play, the implications of which are presented more fully than ever before, and which provides a central image with ramifications everywhere throughout the narrative. Another way of looking at *As You*

Like It and *Twelfth Night* is that they are final and successful testings of the soundness as structural patterns in comedy of the love-game conventions, especially the school of love that leads to the openly acknowledged compact of marriage based upon the freely given pledge of honor and love.

The entire Globe audience knew, as the whole Renaissance had learned from Castiglione, that aspiring youth was powerless without proper education. Thus, we should hear with sympathy Orlando's complaint that his older brother has denied him proper education, a sentiment certain to evoke the sympathetic concern of the London audience, gentleman and commoner, whose faith in the moral efficacy of schooling was as unbounded as that of any humanist schoolteacher. But the name and reputation of gentleman in the world of comedy or, for that matter, in the actual society of the Renaissance, were impossible of attainment without mastery of the code of polite love. Therefore, the school in which Orlando matriculates is not a Platonic Academy for training in adventuring to the realm of the ideal nor a Gresham College where he might learn more about managing his day-by-day fortunes. For, on discovering a likely tutor in Rosalind, disguised as the page Ganymede, he plunges into the curriculum of the school of love with its familiar instruction in the commandments of love. And the audience, of course, expects a display of the jests and wordplay, quibbles, and mannerisms that compose so much of this sequence of studies.

This school of love is held in formal session by Corin and Silvius, who have as their first pupil Rosalind. Rosalind's character has been already defined by her courageous, witty exchanges with Duke Frederick; hence, no further time need be spent in ascribing to her the attributes of the lady of conventional romance. Shakespeare knows that his audience in turn knows that such heroines have certain prerogatives, but in an even more skillful way than in the earlier comedies, he introduces the note of humorous mockery and light-hearted skepticism that sets off in relief the deep trust in the soundness of the conventional relationships of lovers embodied in the feudal and religious metaphor of the sovereign lady.

Rosalind is an apt pupil in the school of love, for merely in overhearing Silvius's virtuosity in his lament for Phebe, a masterly improvisation with pastoral elaboration of the conventional theme of forsaken love, she learns her own sorrow:

> Alas, poor shepherd! searching of thy wound
> I have by hard adventure found mine own.
>
> [II.iv.42–43]

The jests that are a vital part of the tradition when there is a likely clown about follow hard upon Rosalind's confession. No sooner has she spoken then Touchstone reminisces about his love woes and early schooling in the art of *fin amour:* "I remember when I was in love and broke my sword upon a stone, and bid him take that for coming a-night to Jane Smile . . . we that are true lovers run into strange capers" (II.iv.44–46, 52–53). As the school of love progresses, Touchstone carries on a course of instruction parallel to Rosalind's pedagogy. We hear, for example, another set of instructions delivered by him to Audrey, a deplorable student, who fails her examinations. She is, nevertheless, given passing grades by Touchstone, who seems not to mind this lowering of standards. We see once more how such juxtapositions of humor and romance prevent the courtly conventions from offending by becoming a travesty of real persons' emotions, as they might if taken too seriously. Shakespeare proves once more that comic relief is as useful in romantic comedy as in tragedy.

As You Like It uses the school-of-love conventions as at once framework and controlling image, the mold and content of the drama. Rosalind's jesting use of the school-of-love vocabulary, for example, has a dual effect: it amuses by its wit, and it advances the play toward the full completion of the tradition—the lady leads and encourages and judges her lover, accepting him only when he is proved worthy by tests of honor and devotion. Not a bad morality for any era, and certainly a source of lively characterization for Shakespeare in his time.

Rosalind, furthermore, proves to be a diligent as well as humorous schoolmaster, promising to effect Orlando's cure, an offer which Orlando rejects, for the true lover cherishes his

malady. She then gives him some lessons in applied courtship
by posing as his lady; he can, in short, practice his assignments
with her. But she insists that no one has ever died of
love, surely a curious way for a romantic heroine to speak. Her
mockery has been taken to be Shakespeare's own judgment
that the love game is nonsense which sensible grown-ups ought
properly to scorn. This cannot, however, be a correct view, for
Rosalind's jests are not mockery of the conventions but devices
to add zest to the love game. Disguised as Ganymede she can,
of course, say many things that she could not in her proper person. Like any schoolmaster mindful of Erasmus's precepts, she
sets exercises so as to spur her student to greater effort.
By coaching him in the role of lover, she ensures his returning
for more lessons in the art of courtship.

Rosalind is an aggressive heroine, jealous of her prerogatives and surely as anxious as Shakespeare himself to preserve
the integrity of romance. Indeed, the play is remarkable for its
elaborate defenses of the romance conventions, defenses
which are in effect shrewd hits against denigrators of the old
tradition. Shakespeare's handling of the pastoral conventions,
for example, is much like his use of the courtly conventions in
that he hedges them about with the safeguards of humor that
deflect incredulity for the time that the audience is in the theater. Humble Corin's debate with Touchstone gives us the comedy that enlists our sympathies on behalf of Arden by frankly
stating the difference between it and actuality, thus preventing
our having to take pastoralism literally. Again, Jaques, the conventional melancholiac, allows us to take sides for Arden
against him. He is useful as the butt of humorous disdain from
other characters and from the audience as well.

Despite these safeguards that should help us sojourn at
our ease in Arden, an occasional critic still echoes Shaw's objections summarized in his doubly underlining the "You" in *As
You Like It*, implying that Shakespeare was merely pandering
to a public taste that he would, if he were a braver dramatist,
have condemned. Such criticisms are the result, of course, of
a modern unawareness that the conventions of romance are integral parts of the construction and not merely ornaments

added to the story. Thus critics are left with the dilemma of saying something respectful about Shakespeare and at the same time revelatory of their caution lest they be taken in by shoddy goods masquerading under the quality label of Shakespeare's authorship. Lacking anything truly relevant to say, they have recourse to wit as a substitute for criticism, as did the critic who said of *As You Like It* on its production in 1950 in New York that the cluttered stage endangered Rosalind's handsome legs, which "deserve every protection," but the play nevertheless showed evidence of Shakespeare's "matchless genius."[1]

Feeling this way about Shakespeare's romances, Shaw and the antibardolater faction dismiss the whole lot of romantic comedies as Shakespeare's selling out, a waste of genius that could better have been devoted to the improvement of the social order than in maundering about an Arden that never existed anyway. Others, less irate, find that Shakespeare gradually leads his auditory toward the real world of nonconvention, nonromance, nonpastoral, and at the end of the play ever so gently prepares us for the departure from the theater and its Arden and for the return to normality. Can one, however, really believe that whereas Arden is merely a world of fancy, the Court of Duke Frederick represents this world? Common sense tells us that it does not. Two members of that "real world" of Duke Frederick's court—two villains, not just one—are, for instance, seized by conventional repentance. This is the kind of thing that can happen only in romance where it is, truly, normal behavior. Thus the court and the greenwood are wholly within the realm of romance, and the journey from Arden is hardly a return from Arcadia; it is merely a journey from one point to another well within the world of romance. The court where, Duke Senior promises, all "shall share the good of our returned fortunes" is hardly in any country of this world.

Where then is the contact with actuality, where the relevance of romance to life? In part, at least, it is attained through the conventions which project a part of actuality, the wishes, desires, hopes, and morality of normal people, into some kind of traditional form. Mocking clown and jesting

Rosalind are Shakespeare's subtle devices to preserve that
tradition by keeping it at a safe distance and at the same time
inducing us to welcome its relevancy not to the everyday world
of social actuality but to the world of our everyday better
nature.

More important in this play, however, as a way of main-
taining the relevance of romance is the masque of Hymen,
which has a double function. It ensures comfortingly that, of
course, every Jack shall have his Jill, that all ends as "you" like
it; but it also has a dramatic purpose in arriving at a sound,
conclusive ending. This is not to say that Shakespeare himself
necessarily approved of this ending with wedding bells, for he
may quite possibly have maintained an ethical neutrality on
the matter. In the theater, however, there is a tranquil finality
(the proper conclusion of comedy according to Heywood, who
cites Donatus)[2] to romances that end in marriage, for, in this
instance, the school of love, the basic convention in the play,
has achieved good results from its apt pupils. Lessons are, so
to speak, completed, tasks finished, rewards distributed. There
is indeed modesty in the way in which Shakespeare uses the
masque (certainly not a startling innovation in his time) and
cunning in the manner of his employing the masque as confirmation of the final choices made by the characters in the play.
The masque gives completion, as far as dramatic action is concerned; it also renders the narrative delightful instruction in
the code of manners and motives approved of by Everyman in
the audience. But it is also a reenactment of a ritual that under
one guise or another reappears in every age, ensuring the on-
goingness of society. There is a mysterious suprarational connection with nature (surely the Globe audience could sense
it), as Hymen, "god of every town," sings,

> Then is there mirth in heaven
> When earthly things made even
> Atone together.
>   [V.iv.114–16]

  Twelfth Night, or What You Will is also frequently cited
as a case in point by those who want to believe that
Shakespeare so playfully tossed and gored the romantic con-

ventions that they expired. The skeptical mind doubly under-
lines the "You" in *What You* [not I] *Will*, and thus separates
Shakespeare from his audience, seeing him in this play as
again a reluctant entertainer.

At first glance this point of view has some merit, receiving
apparent warrant from Duke Orsino's remarkable display of
petrarchismo. He likes to refer to love as "the rich golden
shaft" and murmurs of love as he reclines on sweet beds of
flowers. This pretty nonsense, however, is not a mockery of the
convention so much as it is a revelation of the kind of person
the duke is at the beginning of the play, an enthusiastic
aesthete. Such deportment, however, is not good dramatic
stuff for romantic comedy if indulged in by more than the one
person it serves to characterize. More than one Duke Orsino
in the play and it might become farce or satire. But Shakespeare is not composing Molièresque farce in the manner of
Les Précieuses ridicules. For there is, after all, a difference between the duke's affectation and his sterner nature, revealed
when he suspects betrayal by Cesario. The true object of ridi-
cule in this as in other romantic comedies is he who despite his
efforts is unfitted by class and temperament to know the art of
courtly love. And the duke is certainly not such a person.

Twelfth Night is, of course, a companion piece to *As You
Like It*. Both are grounded in the school-of-love conventions,
conventions which, incidentally, are substantially present in
their sources. Shakespeare seems not to care, however, that the
source for *As You Like It* has some literary merit whereas the
source of *Twelfth Night* has very little. He chooses stories
without respect to their intrinsic merit, as if he were more attracted by their susceptibility to having their conventional
content reshaped into successful plays. Especially does this
seem true of source stories which hint of possible adaptation
to the school-of-love or the court-of-love conventions, which
serve as narrative framework and offer ready-made motivations
and stereotype characterizations liable to deft alteration or
ironic inversion. The narrative scheme implicit in the school-
of-love aspects of romantic comedy governs almost automatically the selection of scenes and characters from the lengthy
source story. It goes without saying that ill-devised plays could

be fashioned from the rambling stories of Lodge and Rich. Many of Shakespeare's contemporaries wrote diffuse and rambling dramas, concentration and compression not being outstanding traits of Elizabethan writers. In contrast, we see Shakespeare using the conventions as aids in the compressing of episodic, protracted narratives into a unity of action.

The familiar conventions of the school of love and the code of conduct incumbent upon the lover contribute unity of action to *Twelfth Night*. They serve, for example, to develop the relationships between the duke and Viola. Whereas in *As You Like It* Orlando was the pupil, eager to learn from the skillful instructor Ganymede, Orsino is well versed in the code and prides himself on his mastery of the art of love. The ingenuity of having the instructor instructed can then serve as witty conclusion to the romance and as a restorer of proper relationships. At the beginning of the play he gives lessons to Viola, whose disguise, like Rosalind's, adds a pretty diversion. For the code proper forbids the lady to be the aggressor; she has to wait until the feudal metaphor is acted out, with the man professing himself her servant. Then she must for a while affect disdain before, convinced of his worth, she at last grants him her love. Given a suitable disguise, however, the romantic heroine can act not freely but according to the conventions of a role appropriate to her disguise. Because of its ironic contradiction of her "true" status this disguise can be a source of comedy or pathos. In the situation in which she finds herself at the duke's court, for instance, Viola can direct considerable attention to herself without immodesty, but she must remain, in the actuality which is how the playwright intends us to see the duke's court, true servant to the duke. Orlando, fortunately for Rosalind, was cast in the proper role from the beginning as servant-lover to Ganymede-Rosalind in their pretended courtship. But Viola, like Julia in *Two Gentlemen*, is servant to him who should be servant to her. The disguise being dropped, there is a flurry of rearranging relationships, of recalling the proper, accepted conventions and reaffirming their correctness, and all ends well, to the plighting of marriage troths of course, as Viola reigns "Orsino's mistress and his fancy's queen."

The school-of-love metaphor with its attendant feudal metaphor invites, as Shakespeare learned to his profit in the early comedies, a parody in the subplot. Whereas Viola, merely pretending to be a servant, can engage in *fin amour* as benefits her true social rank, Malvolio, really a servant, becomes ridiculous when he attempts to play the role of love servant to the lady Olivia, misreading and misapplying the lesson of love in his opportunistic and hypocritical attempt to play a courtly role. Puritanically minded opportunists must, of course, be chastised for their attempted intrusion into romance.

Malvolio, incidentally, is undone by his recognizing that the letter concocted by Maria and Sir Toby to bait their trap is a correct summary of love conventions, as indeed it is; it speaks accurately of the secrecy of love, "No man must know"; it reminds him of the irony of his inferior status and of the proper relationship of lady and lover, "I may command where I adore." Vain Malvolio resents the rule of love which would make him doubly subject to Olivia's command; nevertheless, he will exert himself to please her fancy for yellow hose, cross-gartered.

Having so thoroughly exploited the school-of-love convention in these two plays, Shakespeare will the more readily turn to other resources—because he wants to, not because he is compelled to attempt satire and tragicomedy in order to compete with other playwrights, Beaumont and Fletcher, for example. Shakespeare, moreover, seems not to have been attracted, as Beaumont and Fletcher and others were, by the easy way to success through mockery of the conventions themselves. He mocks the mockers and misusers and abusers of the conventions, not the conventions themselves. Hence, the fully developed parody of the subplot of *Twelfth Night*. The wooer in the old dispensation was obliged to demonstrate his prowess by deeds of valor in order to win his lady. The Renaissance demanded that in addition he display skill in letters and music. Thus, Sir Andrew, that accomplished knight, becomes a parody of the witty gentleman courtier-wooer of the courtesy books and the choicer novels of love. Alas, the poor fellow's back trick, which he has "simply as strong as any man in Illyria," is not enough. He tries, nevertheless, at the urging of Sir Toby, to prove his worth in the more old-fashioned way of defeating his rival in a passage of arms, which, fortunately for the outcome of the play, serves to reveal the true identities of Sebastian and Viola.

The school-of-love pattern has a built-in narrative pattern and is, consequently, easily dramatized. The court of love, on the other hand, provides a situation but little action, while the religion-of-love metaphor provides means of characterization and some narrative possibility. The three go together quite well, and in the fully developed romantic pattern of the last plays they are used cooperatively. In the Globe period, from 1600 to 1610, however, we find Shakespeare first using in his comedies the school of love and then employing, in *All's Well that Ends Well*, the court-of-love situation with its concomitant *débat* and characterizations derived from the religion-of-love metaphor. The situation of the last scene, for instance, which takes place in the king's court, turns upon the debate on love and honor. This was undoubtedly suggested by the source, the tale of Giletta of Narbonne, which Shakespeare got in the main from Painter's translation of Boccaccio's story. The source follows a simple narrative pattern, the same that guides the play. But Shakespeare, employing the religion-of-love metaphor, introduces implications which draw the play to different conclusions and lead to greater involvement on the part of the audience.

All's Well is reminiscent of *Two Gentleman* in its interweaving of the religion of love, the code of the lover, and the contention between love and honor. The definition of these opposing forces takes up most of the play, leading up to the judgment given, appropriately, before the king in what is, in effect, a court of love, the king having earlier ordered Bertram's marriage and now being called upon to judge the validity of the consummation of that marriage. At first, the play seems to promise merely the mild surprise (for an audience expecting that an advertised comedy would of course be a story of wooing and winning) of beholding once more the lady as wooer in some sort of disguise. What surprises and annoys us is Bertram's complete and sinful unworthiness until he is repentant and redeemed at the very last minute. With *All's Well* Shakespeare again tests (as he did in *Two Gentlemen*) the religion-of-love convention as if trying to see how much stress it can bear as a structural element of drama.

In *All's Well*, moreover, characters such as forgiving (and pursuing) woman and reluctant, detestable, but at the last minute repentant, therefore worthy, hero derive their validity not from realistic psychology but from the religion-of-love convention with its customary last-minute repentances—a mode of dramatic address that may have lost its savor for the present-day theatergoer but was for the Globe audience altogether worthy of approval. But even a modern audience readily concedes that Helena's love is genuine and she is pathetically forlorn when she speaks, in the accents of a devotee of the religion of love, after Bertram's departure from Rossillion: "But now he's gone, and my idolatrous fancy must sanctify his relics" (I.i.108–9). The pathos of this must strike us, though the metaphor is alien.

Lest she be inhibited by the idolatry accorded women in the old religion, Helena, like other of Shakespeare's heroines, assumes disguises which permit her native shrewdness and practicality fuller scope. Nor is Helena wanly and retiringly virtuous. She has, after all, been under the tutelage of the countess and has acquired sufficient nobility of manner and address. She is, in effect, a character fashioned according to literary convention. Hence the paradoxes of the servant-lover relationship are naturally part of her vocabulary when, in alarm at the prospect of the countess's suggesting that she regard Bertram with sisterly affection, she replies, not daring to confess more,

> My master, my dear lord he is; and I
> His servant live, and will his vassal die:
> He must not be my brother
>
> [I.iii.164–66]

The countess, shrewdly catching the meaning of the feudal metaphor of the courtly love language, knows what is in Helena's mind and encourages her to establish the right relationship. The problem, as the audience must see it, is to arrange matters so the highborn Bertram will become vassal-in-love to Helena. This metamorphosis occurs in two stages: first is Helena's pursuit of Bertram, a hunting down of the sinner, as it were, by modesty and yielding, typical of Shakespeare's fondness for the paradox that catches the auditory's ear by its strangeness, but ends by reaffirming the moral soundness of such conventions as the religion-of-love metaphor. The second stage in Bertram's correction is the revelation of Helena's successful imposition of her sway over his honor, and this is told before the king in the concluding court of love.

Bertram, Count of Rossillion, seems a most unworthy object of Helena's pursuit. Proud, arrogant, willing to lie, devoted to a specious concept of honor—what a man to be beloved by Helena, whom Shakespeare has so plentifully endowed with beauty, wit, and, most important, determination. Consequently, not many of us think that this play, despite its title, does end well. For admirers of romantic heroines find that Helena is mistreated and romantic comedy itself travestied. On the other hand, those who, finding romantic comedy merely a compound of nonsensical transvestism and improbable story, interpret Shakespeare's earlier comedies as his iconoclastic effort to rid the stage of such trash deem this play unsatisfactory because it is clumsily done; its attack lacks cutting edge. Only those who would make of Shakespeare's romances paradigms of Christian theology wholeheartedly admire the play. Their view, liable as it is to attack by those who commonsensically want to keep Shakespeare in the theater and out of the pulpit, is nevertheless nearer the truth than that of the denigrators.

Most of the difficulties concerning interpretation of the play will be met if we keep in mind that Shakespeare is dealing first of all with dramaturgy, not with psychology or theology. He is preparing for the climax of the play where he will try to save the day, dramatically speaking, by drawing upon the vital connection between the religion-of-love conventions and the court of love, that is, the familiar "fact" of the ennobling quality of love. There are implications in this, a welcome surplus of meanings that accrue to the conventions when well-handled, that need not be termed sententiously Shakespeare's "philosophy." This is not to say that Shakespeare was careless of such effects or that he let anagogical implications surprise himself as well as the audience. He was aware of the implications of the metaphors he used, and he found a way to make the formal conventions speak more eloquently in their own terms, thus more provocatively, than mere exegesis could hope to on ethical and religious matters.

Bertram can thus be aptly termed a sinner against love, a rebel against grace—phrases which pertain alike to the religion of romantic love and to theology. The more desperate the case, the more remarkable the cure; and Bertram is initially far more steeped in sin than the usual converted scoffer at love. He is an adept at the love game, who, having sinned against the god of love, must yield at last to the pursuing grace tendered by Helena, the agent of the god.

In conflict with Helena's tender of honorable love is Bertram's quest for honor in the Italian wars. For him, the pursuit of honor is an escape from the service of virtuous love and not a proving of himself so as to be worthy of his lady. As we might have supposed from our by now considerable acquaintance with the romance conventions, a youth like Bertram who makes facile distinctions between love and honor proves more a cavalier of the balcony and bedchamber than of the battlefield. He delights in exhibiting his adeptness in the art of wooing, employing the terms of the old tradition, even as he uses the language of honor, as betrayals of his own vows and the commands of his king. He protests to Diana, for example, that the object of his allegiance must be of his own choosing, and, invoking the most troublesome precept of courtly romance, assures Diana that love in marriage is impossible:

> I was compell'd to her; but I love thee
> By love's own sweet constraint, and will forever
> Do thee all rights of service.
>
> [IV.ii.15–17]

The tone is right; the words sort well; the metaphor is correct. The trouble is that these are the words of a moral knave, a man in need of some kind of rescue. How appropriate it is, then, that immediately after the widow's caution to Diana against the kind of love proffered by Bertram through the intermediary, "filthy officer" Parolles, Helena should appear in the guise of a pilgrim. The metaphor of the religion of love is fully acted out. And for Bertram, the sinner enamored of his sin, cure is at hand.

So ardent a believer in the code of courtly love is Bertram that he must at last be trapped by the true meaning implicit in the protestations of faith required by the code. The paradox reads like a homily. Faithful to the dictates of the love conventions, Bertram surrenders his whole being to Diana when he gives her the symbolic pledge:

> Here, take my ring;
> My house, mine honor, yea, my life be thine,
> And I'll be bid by thee.
>
> [IV.ii.52–54]

Now his very life is at the lady's disposal, her power over him as complete as that of any lady of medieval romance over her knight. When Diana asserts this authority over Bertram later in the king's court, he will at last have been saved.

The last act takes cognizance of all of these issues and submits their arbitrament to the king, whose sifting of evidence and final judgment sort neatly with the court-of-love motif. The arguments of plaintiff and defendant, a cause to be adjudicated, the exhibits of the two rings as symbols of love and honor (and conversely of Bertram's broken vows and tarnished honor)—all of these are involved in Diana's accusation, which asserts the priority of the lady's honor that Bertram unwittingly swore to uphold.

The play's culmination in Bertram's sudden change from arrogant defiance to repentant gratitude is perfectly explicable by ascribing, as tradition does, a redeeming quality to love. If this be nonsense according to the experience of actual men and women, it is nevertheless the best of sense according

to the romance tradition which reflects, in psychologically correct generalizations, the vagaries of human nature. Penitent
and forgiven in a moment, Bertram must be regarded as restored to moral health even as Proteus in *Two Gentlemen* or
Oliver in *As You Like It*. They are all creatures of the same
convention, but the plays which they inhabit are variously
judged, with *As You Like It* usually faring better than the
other two.

A further reason that *All's Well* takes second place to *As
You Like It* in modern esteem is that repentant sinner Bertram
is a major figure, whereas the repentant villains Oliver and
Frederick are minor figures—even though the happy outcome
of the play springs from their conversion. Modern audiences
find it as difficult to pardon Bertram as to forgive Proteus and
are offended at his apparently undeserved good fortune. But
of equal importance in the higher esteem accorded *As You
Like It* is its better employment of humor. The usual codas of
humorous mockery of the conventions seem only offhandedly
done in *All's Well*, not directly pertinent to the principal business. Thus, the clown's stock parodies of the conventions, his
confession that his melancholy springs from his having lost
his taste for "Isbels o' the country," is poor stuff compared with
Touchstone's lively schoolmastership in the art of love. Similarly, Parolles has too much on his raffish mind to be wholly in
point in the love-game aspects of the play. His role of braggart
warrior and Vice affords commentary on Bertram's valor, but
he is too much a figure of satire, with too much independence
of judgment to be acclimated in romance, and this affects the
tone of the play in a manner not altogether pleasant.

The comedies of the Globe period come in pairs, each pair
based on a set of conventions which guide the narrative and
embody the theme, and each pair constituting both test and
affirmation of the conventions. Each pair, moreover, represents
Shakespeare's final concentration upon its particular sets of
conventions. *As You Like It* and *Twelfth Night* employ the
school of love as basic convention; *All's Well* and *Measure for
Measure* are based on the allied conventions of the religion
of love for theme and the court of love for bringing the narra-

tive to a close. The two earlier comedies are well-nigh perfect versions of their conventions; nothing more could be added. But the religion-of-love metaphor has implications which Shakespeare finds difficult fully to express in dramatic form until his last plays. Hence the comparative lack of success on stage of *All's Well* and *Measure for Measure* as compared with perennial joyful triumphs of the earlier comedies. One reason for this is, of course, that the dramatic metaphors of the school of love involve primarily social deportment and are easier to comprehend. Stories of the correction of scoffers at love's power are more easily told. But sinners and hypocrites are the true enemies and subverters of love in the metaphor of the religion of love. They bring about more than just the unhappiness of youthful lovers, for they are subverters of *all* good. In the old dispensation, we must believe that love is everything good in the world even as love of God is everything good in eternity. Angelo, deputy to Duke Vincentio, would not have made a travesty of the ruler's obligation to mete out impartial justice, for example, had he not first played false to love's holy vows.

The cynical jest that forever threatens the courtly tradition is suggested in *Measure for Measure* as it is in *All's Well*: in bed all women are the same. To the cynical mind, moreover, there is no such thing as love at first sight, but there is lust at first sight, the reverse of love's bright coinage. Hence, all vows of fidelity, protestations of honor, worship of the lady, risking one's life in her service, all the paraphernalia of the code of love, in short, are but a catalog of ridiculous aberration written across the pages of western literature and infecting with hypocrisy the lives of men and women who should know better. In *Measure for Measure* this cynicism is given full expression and, by a remarkable dramatic tour de force, defeated. It is another example of Shakespeare's respect for his audience that he attempts to bring this triumph off over the most adverse odds and does not insult his hearers' intelligence by knocking down enfeebled ideas.

The persecution of the bawds of Vienna is a grotesquely appropriate background for Angelo's ensnarement in lust for

the particular body. His lust is paradoxically exorcized by in-
dulgence that mocks it: Mariana or Isabella, Diana or Helena
—without the traditional religion of love there is no difference,
as lust-driven Angelo and Bertram both discover. It is, after
all, not the body of love that matters but the abstraction, the
ideal, that enhances the body. Thus Angelo falls into the grav-
est sin of the old religion, confusing love and lust, which is,
to use the old-fashioned language, love without honor. And
thus it is that Proteus, equally guilty for his threats to ravish
Silvia but being, for the most part, conventional scoffer at the
power of love, is never taken seriously; but Angelo, deeply involved in the religion of love, can be regarded as a profound
study of the fragility of a merely formal, therefore hypocritical, virtue.

The metaphor of the religion of love requires or leads
easily to characterizations of saints and sinners. Angelo is
among the sinners, or better yet, among the apostates. Among
the other ramifications of the metaphor as it spreads to encom-
pass the whole play are the characterizations of Duke
Vincentio and Isabella. Hear, for example, the duke's testy
reply to Friar Thomas's supposition that the duke retreats from
the world for the sake of love, some secret amour perhaps (as
if he were entering upon a life of contemplation and prayer to
the god of love):

> No holy father! throw away that thought;
> Believe not that the dribbling dart of love
> Can pierce a complete bosom.
>
> [I.iii.1–3]

It is fitting that in this strange world of Vienna peopled by
saints and sinners, all obsessed with love and its metaphorical
expression in the traditional forms of the religion of love, the
duke should take the cowl as disguise and refuge from love.
On the other hand, he who scoffs at the power of love, "the
dribbling dart of love," must, by all the experienced anticipa-
tions of the audience, end a convert to love, as indeed he does,
choosing by another appropriate turn of the metaphor, to ven-
erate the "ensky'd saint" Isabella.

The duke is one of the most enigmatic of Shakespeare's characters—not because his thoughts are profound or his psychology inordinately complex. Such impressions arise, as we have already seen in Shakespeare's apprentice plays, when two or more stereotypes are joined in one. Thus with the duke, and Hamlet also. The duke as convert to the religion of love must bear some marks of the hero of romance, but these are evident only at the beginning and end of the play in a line or two which, however, occasion more explaining away by modern writers than any other aspect of this problem play. Then, after playing the role of intriguer, Duke Vincentio suddenly becomes a devotee to love and marriage, a change hardly explicable save by reference to convention, when it becomes the only truly appropriate ending.

Measure for Measure suffers from present-day lack of appreciative understanding; we see in it problems that are not really there. Certainly the term "problem play" would have puzzled the Globe audience. The "problem" for us springs from two sources: one is our insensitivity to the metaphors of the religion-of-love conventions—we could do better in seeing their relevances to the whole play, to be sure, but this would require a conscious effort that the Globe auditory, because of its familiarity with the whole set of conventions, must have been spared. The other is our preoccupation with the political dilemma, the question of the use and misuse of power. To an audience familiar with the *Mirror for Magistrates* none of Angelo's or Escalus's speeches would have posed any difficulty or have seemed extraordinary. We pay too much attention to Angelo as political figure and not enough to him as sinner in the religion of love. Actually he is a mouther of political commonplaces. But we insist on viewing him as the central figure in an edificatory play about the problems of managing both individual men and a commonwealth given to violent fluctuations between profligacy and puritanism.

The play is, however, nicely balanced. Its themes find expression in the conventions appropriate on the one hand to the political play (good and evil counselors, the wicked magistrate, the official voice of political order, and so on) and, on the other, to the romance centered on the religion of love. The real problem of *Measure for Measure* for Shakespeare was not so much the moral implications of the narrative as how to combine the two sets of conventions in a dramatic structure. This joining he tries to effect with the same trick he used in the English history plays: a Vice figure that can infiltrate both "plots," adopt disguises to control and outwit all other characters, stir up trouble, yet be accepted as friend and counselor by all. As contriver of plots, observer, counselor to both sides in the conflict, Vincentio has some of the function and attributes of the Vice. He is a tempter of men, but to virtue rather than evil. Like Helena in the companion play *All's Well*, he is a paradoxical reversal or inversion of a stock character. He deceives men into goodness; he lies to Claudio, eavesdrops on Isabella and Claudio, and baits the trap for the villain.

Lucio is the more ordinary Vice, of course, and licensed commentator. Yet even in his character there is an overplus. Other Vices merely comment on the wickedness of tyrants, but Lucio's role leads him to do something in behalf of the victims of tyranny. It is from Lucio, after all, that we hear the memorable description of Isabella, "a thing ensky'd and sainted." And were it not for him, Claudio would have been early lost. For Isabella is ready to approve Angelo's condemnation and is ready to abandon her appeal for clemency for her brother. Repeatedly Lucio pushes her back to plead again with Angelo: "Give'st not o'er so: to him again, entreat him!" (II.ii.43).

One further comment about the play: Shakespeare finds it convenient to end the drama with the same gathering up of issues and judgments as in *All's Well*. Undiscovered and secret motives are revealed, all of the errors and hypocrisies perpetrated in the name of love set forth. It is fitting, therefore, to think of Vincentio as presiding over what is in effect a court of love and distributing rewards and punishments according to the tenets of the religion of love. Vincentio himself then subscribes to the sweet and comfortable doctrines prescribed by that religion to which Isabella is also converted. The religion-of-love metaphor throws light upon the happenings in Vienna's courts, byways, and prisons, and allows us to see farther into the play itself than from any other vantage point.

In moving to the Globe, Shakespeare put behind him, for the most part, the subject of English history, which had been one of the staples of his apprenticeship. Comparatively easy to construct and easily filled with acceptable moral and political edification, the history play lent itself to his search for fame and, more importantly, to his quest for expertness in play construction. Shakespeare found chronicle both easy to master and suited to considerable experimentation. But English history ceased to be current popular dramatic fare by the end of the decade of the nineties, and the writers for the Chamberlain's Men at the new Globe turned eagerly to Roman history as a storehouse of material affording the same combination of celebrated and edificatory subject matter.

Sir Thomas North, when he placed his translation of Plutarch firmly within the Renaissance tradition of useful and delightful literature, felt himself benefactor to his age: "Among all profane books that are in reputation at this day there is none that teaches so much honor, love, obedience, reverence, zeal, and devotion to princes as these *Lives* of Plutarch do." How then could Shakespeare, any more than his audience, have failed to regard accounts of Caesar's life as primarily instructive. Shakespeare could not possibly, as has been asserted, have taken Plutarch's account of Caesar simply as a well-told narrative susceptible to effective dramatization for the theater of 1599.[3] The rendering of the political edification of any of Plutarch's biographies into acceptable dramatic fare would have been easy for Shakespeare. But to look at Plutarch's *Lives* and choose someone other than Caesar as the primary example of the tragedies of great men and great states would hardly have occurred to any Renaissance mind.

Shakespeare brings Caesar's story to the stage by employing the conventions of the history play and revenge play, to which are added an extraordinary number of conventional references to the natural correspondences that lend, as happens in English history plays and in the tragedies, dignity and consequence to the narrative and dramatic liveliness to the edification. Indeed, the amount of obvious edification in *Caesar* and in the other Roman plays gives the lie to Dr. Johnson's statement that Shakespeare would rather delight than instruct. Nevertheless, the edification in *Caesar*, because it has been made an integral part of the play's structure, is, compared with history written by other hands, ambiguous, being on the one hand received political opinion and on the other becoming a test of simplified judgments on politics or human nature.

A multiple aim, then, governs the selection of incident and character from Plutarch's lengthy accounts of Caesar and Brutus. Caesar, for example, is shown to be a compendium of the traits, both good and bad, that traditionally characterize monarchs in the history plays. He uses the tone and vocabulary of an arbitrary, proud monarch when, seated in the Senate, he invites petitions and is surrounded by courtiers and suitors. "I am constant as the northern star," he intones, and the metaphor implies that nature itself is a projection of men's political affairs. Caesar as the constant star around which the ordered heavens revolve would, of course, suggest to the Globe audience the same political doctrine that gave support to the English history plays, namely the medieval and Renaissance assumptions that the ruler was the very center of the state and all order dependent upon him. But when Caesar makes of this teaching a personal boast, the state is imperiled by his pride that makes him liable to Decius's flattering deceit and to unwise counselors like Antony, whose only advice is "Fear him not, Caesar."

The natural portents, a major convention of the play, confer dignity upon Caesar's tragedy. Despite the obvious relevancy of the tempest to Caesar's fate and to the fate of great Rome itself, however, everyone in the play either misreads or ignores portents whose significances to anyone in the Globe audience must have been as clear as the lightning flashes which illuminate Brutus's perusal of the false and flattering letters concocted by Cassius. Too little of sophisticated dramatic irony in this, perhaps, which suggests why *Caesar* is of lesser excellence compared with *Lear*. The truthful portents that bode disaster to the ruler of the state, hence to the state itself, can by wise men be read aright.

Caesar's pride, as has been noted, makes him seem a pettier figure than a great man should be; hence, the modern mind especially has difficulty in determining the relative statures of Caesar and Brutus, suspecting that the play should by right be entitled *The Tragedy of Marcus Brutus*, but all the while failing to appreciate the enormity of Brutus's crime. For Brutus is no more skillful in reading portents than Caesar. They are grave, he acknowledges, but he is oblivious to what they presage. The Globe audience could undoubtedly tell that a character so blind must be the victim of his own proud self-assurance.

The principal edification contained in Brutus's career is simple. The rebel against order is automatically an inspirer of disorder. A chance exists that the rebel may impose an order of his own on the state, but it is a slim chance, won only seldom, as by Bolingbroke and then actually for a brief time until sufficient retribution is visited upon a succeeding generation in the turmoil of the Wars of the Roses, hints of which disaster are plentifully strewn throughout the *Henry IV* plays. Brutus has neither Bolingbroke's cause nor ability. Much given to political maxims, he resembles a conner of bits from the *Mirror for Magistrates*, in which treatise destroyers of order are always, no matter what their motives, guarantors of disorder.

Such characters (in order to function efficiently as part of the play's structure) traditionally require a counselor-confidant. Plutarch furnishes Cassius for this role, and Shakespeare finds him so well fitted that he needs not much adaptation, save for the emphasis put upon his activities as intriguer. Surprises, however, await us in this Vice figure who counsels people to their own ruin, for although he does not want his "victim" ruined, such is the result. Cassius's devices for hoodwinking Brutus are, nevertheless, stock-in-trade for any stage Machiavellian. Add, then, the further complication of the same intriguer's later sound advice and commonsense practice before Philippi being rejected by his former dupe, and we have the elements of the familiar debate between friendship and honor intensified to the point of life-and-death decisions.

A play beginning with plots and murders must necessarily, on the Elizabethan stage, conform somewhat to the revenge-play pattern. Both tragedy and the chronicle play can readily adopt the formal structure of the blood-revenge plot, and *Caesar* employs this familiar continuity in yet another sequence of balances: the correspondences providing doctrinal instruction in the harmony of nature and the ordered state, the revenge motif working in a series of tensions against that background. A redoubled instructiveness thus informs the play —a far cry indeed from its being merely an interesting narrative readily adaptable to the stage—for in addition to fulfilling the politically instructive aim that any play involving Caesar would be expected to convey, it instructs morally, and for us perhaps platitudinously, by showing murder avenged. For the Elizabethans, however, such instructiveness, far from being platitudinous, was so involved both with politics and the code of personal honor that its dramatization was naturally a pattern for history plays and tragedies.

Antony early in the play assumes the role of avenger, at once given motive and function in his address to Caesar's corpse after the murder. By all custom and expectation, Antony should from this time on in the story be the chief figure. A history play incorporating a revenge plot would usually have it so. But Shakespeare plays it differently, relegating Antony toward the end of the play to a mere companion role to Octavius. Much of the effectiveness of the play derives from such an unexpected turning of a conventional pattern, but it also depends upon retaining the conventional pattern and characterizations (this done through Antony's speeches promising revenge for Caesar, his behaving like a Machiavellian, and, of course, through having Caesar's ghost walk the encampment at Sardis).

A further subtlety in the use of the conventions is the casting of Brutus as a reluctant and conscientious usurper (modeled on Bolingbroke and in turn providing a model for

Hamlet and Macbeth). Thus *Caesar* is a divided masterpiece, being the last of Shakespeare's great history plays and at the same time the first of the major tragedies. The balance, however, seems to tip somewhat toward history because of its emphasis on the cycle of political order, disorder, and restored order. It is not wholly revenge tragedy because, among other possible examples, Antony's role as avenger is diminished by the intrusion of Octavius and, more importantly, because of the truncation of the encounter of ghost and murderer, a scene pivotal in the revenge-tragedy genre. Caesar's ghost is a remarkably taciturn specter and, by the standards of Senecan ghost lore, only half-hearted in its attempt to afflict Brutus's conscience. Brutus's slight reaction to the apparition exemplifies Shakespeare's technique at this point, a calculated deception based on the tender to the audience of an expected convention and the immediate snatching back or reversal of the convention. Now you see the revenge-play ghost—now you don't. Hence, the emphasis lights upon Brutus and his indomitability. For the sake of this surprise which characterizes Brutus as calm and resolute though fate-pursued, but so in love with honor that he can admit no blemish in himself, Shakespeare sacrifices considerable accuracy of tone and theme.

In a play profiting from the tradition that history edifies, especially in the accounts of the falls of great men, Shakespeare has, let us put it bluntly, dealt hypocritically. He gives much edification, as expected; but the edification seems to be overlaid with contradictions that only at first glance are subtleties. *Caesar*, beginning in the tradition of the history play as vehicle for political instruction, suggests a revenge play at its end. Accompanying this shift, sometimes hindering, sometimes inspiring, are the conventional multitudinous references to the natural correspondences, the defiances exchanged by the contesting parties, the intrigues, in the manner of the Vice, carried on now by Cassius, now by Antony. The conflict in the play's narrative portion, nevertheless, is fairly well resolved in the achieved revenge for Caesar's death and the meting out to Brutus what the audience would have to agree is perfect justice. But many questions are left open as the result of the collision of conventions and the resultant unresolved tensions, not so much in the narrative pattern as in the theme. What is it, we wonder, that Shakespeare intends? It must be that he wants to have it both ways: a satisfactorily reassuring ending for his tragedy as a moral stage piece, and at the same time a suggestion that the moral dilemma is unending, that man lives forever in a state of moral ambivalence where moral questions are never wholly resolved but will be dealt with again and again—in plays which will await the interested attention of next week's and next month's audiences at the Globe.

No such equivocation affects Jonson's *Sejanus*. In that weighty history the instructive pattern is simply constructed from standard conventions. The lesson is that the state is endangered when wicked counselors have the ruler's ear and trust. The only remedy is for the ruler to gain once more the judicious and searching overview of his realm, as Tiberius does through his letter to the senate, exposing Sejanus and regaining the senate's loyalty. Most of the action of the play, however, is performed by the conventional intriguers, Sejanus and Macro, who maneuver against each other with Machiavellian underhandedness. What we miss in *Sejanus*, in comparison with Shakespeare's Roman plays, is, for one thing, the grander tradition of historical drama embodied in references to the system of natural correspondences. In Jonson's play, such references are at best mere scholarly citations of the auguries, falling far short of any poetic suggestiveness of a destiny that shapes and reflects the fate of empires. Indeed, *Sejanus* is more a classic play of intrigue adapted to tragedy than it is tragedy itself. And its edification is chiefly the trite notion of Fortune's wheel casting down now one, now another aspirant to fame and power.

Begin with the familiar, and without losing sight of it, suggest the new, strange, and hitherto unguessed truth—that is the way to write a successful play. Such seems to be Shakespeare's guiding and continuing principle as he successively combines disparate elements into the alloy that is the tragedy of *Hamlet*. The modern audience can comprehend only in part the precision of Shakespeare's craftsmanship in ringing changes upon what was to the audience of 1602 or 1603 a more than familiar opening pattern. We have to engage in subtleties about willingly suspending our disbelief, whereas for the Globe audience belief or disbelief did not even enter the mind. For instead of being introduced into a strange world of ghost and apparition, the Globe auditor could savor the dispatch with which the narrative is launched into the revenge plot of which a ghost is customary harbinger. It was, therefore, from his superior knowledge that the judicious spectator at the Globe, although acknowledging Horatio's skill in cross-questioning spirits, would observe that Horatio is missing the point in failing to ask the obvious question—which almost any member of the audience could supply. The ghost of Hamlet's father wants to reveal the identity of his murderer. To ask an armed specter other questions is to waste its time.

Horatio's ghost lore, furthermore, impresses upon the audience Hamlet's daring in venturing into a realm beyond our ken. Actually, the Globe audience would have known far more about that realm than the ghost tells. It is reminded of, but not burdened with, the revenge-play commonplaces of the Senecan afterworld. To the connoisseurs of revenge plays and stories, therefore, this must have seemed a most considerate ghost, himself a creature of horror, who does not trouble ears too long assailed (by Andrea's ghost in Kyd's *Spanish Tragedy*, for example) with terrors of Phlegethon and Tartarus. How inconsequential, then, to inquire whether this is a Christian ghost or a folklore ghost. It is, simply, a conventional ghost whose function it is to urge Hamlet to sweep to revenge. But at this moment of recognition of the convention, the unconventional intrudes. Something is added, enriching as well as distorting the familiar pattern as the ghost implicates Gertrude and bids Hamlet, "Leave her to heaven." Not one object of revenge but two are suggested to the revenger Hamlet, and he is forthwith confronted with a problem of moral discrimination such as no other revenger on the Elizabethan stage ever faced.

In his first state of certainty, assuring himself that all he has to do is to destroy the murderer, Hamlet resolves on an obvious tactic, obvious that is to those skilled in revenge-play conventions. He proposes to adopt, as protective camouflage from his enemy, an "antic disposition" that suggests madness, real or pretended. So far an almost simple pattern: ghost, revenger, known murderer, a confidant for the avenger, the hero's antic behavior. Only the nagging "Leave her to heaven" is much out of the ordinary. But the conventional limitations of revenge tragedy are suddenly burst through and other moral vistas suggested when Hamlet becomes a reluctant avenger, thus putting the audience on its mettle to judge him with impatience or with sympathy. We have, then, an apparently reluctant avenger who fancies himself the unwilling minister of justice to his age: "Ah cursed spite, that ever I was born to set it right."

How is Hamlet prepared for these visions of ghostly admonition and moral obligation? And how is the audience induced to accept Hamlet as a welcome—though puzzling—change from the stereotype avenger so strongly suggested in the opening encounter with the ghost? For it is not Shakespeare's habit to spring mere surprises or changes upon his audience, which would only fragment the play and debase and oversimplify the characters, as happens in the fantastic exaggerations of the blood tragedy of Tourneur, Ford, and Webster. Many stage avengers were men of moods, and the melancholiac was no stranger to the Globe auditory. Hamlet is certainly melancholy, but his melancholia expresses itself in references to the traditional natural correspondences. The world is an unweeded garden—evocative metaphor—whence order and stability have fled. This image furnishes the setting of a traditional state play involving evil kings, realms ill governed, and society consequently disordered and diseased. Place in this setting the melodramatic circumstances of a revenge play and we have a play as extensive in scope as any history play or tragedy. This complexity is modestly introduced by Hamlet's musings, and the alloy is fashioned so unobtrusively that similarity to Shakespeare's more obvious joining in *Caesar* of the conventions of the revenge play and history play goes almost unnoticed. In *Hamlet* a better balance is attained. In both plays, as in all of the tragedies, metaphors of the natural correspondences provide the catalyst.

Modesty is the key word for Hamlet's being created the reluctant doer who meditates on justice and fate and self-knowledge. But cunning would be the key word for Hamlet's being created also the skilled avenger. The resultant alloy is given tensile strength through the delineation of the prince's several roles: perfectionist in revenge, Machiavellian in plotting the death of the king's henchmen, and Vice in perpetrating his deceptions of Claudius and Polonius.

The point of greatest tension, when the meditative, visionary youth and the perfectionist, rational avenger are at odds in Hamlet's character, is the moment when he stands behind the praying king—or Hamlet *thinks* the king is praying, whereas we know that Claudius's attempt at prayer is failing—and meditates the immediate dispatch of his enemy. Shakespeare may, of course, have hit upon this scene by happy intuition. More likely, he calculated its effect and knew it would involve the audience in two ways. Caught up in the movement of the play and responding to Hamlet's furious denunciation of the king; satisfied, moreover, by the mousetrap play that Claudius is indeed guilty, the audience to a man wants Hamlet to strike. But the spectacle of a kneeling man's being run through the back must be appalling to all but the most callous, and in the moment of relief that accompanies our realization that Shakespeare (and Hamlet) will spare us this sight, there must occur a twinge, however momentary, of conscience. Especially for the Elizabethan audience would this be so, for the propriety of revenge was a matter of daily argument, and tirades from pulpit and throne denounced and forbade the taking of life in the name of personal honor and vengeance. Thus, the audience is challenged to examine (during the moment of Hamlet's hesitation as he looks at the kneeling king, as well as later in retrospective judgment) the implications of its desire to see Hamlet act, for in so wishing it has sinned against its professed belief in the necessarily evil nature of revenge and against its allegiance to the teachings of church and mon-

arch concerning revenge. It is not only Hamlet's conscience
and Claudius's that are caught in the play.

Not only in the characterization of Hamlet are Shakespeare's artistic modesty and cunning evident but also in the
construction of the play. Shakespeare often uses the same pattern of construction for romantic comedies as for history plays
and tragedies. The opening scene presents a group of characters, a court, for example, and the final scene is a meeting of
a royal court which functions as a court of justice also. The
court is an area for conflict of characters at the beginning of
the play, a setting for the resolution of conflict at the end. This
setting is quite natural as the royal court of the chronicle play,
of course, but it is also used by Shakespeare in romantic comedy as a court of love wherein one in authority metes out rewards and punishments according to the tenets of the commandments of love, where the power of the lord or god of love
is confirmed, and where rebels against love's power are chas-
tened. Borrow this convention from its traditional context of
romance, introduce it into tragedy, and all kinds of innuendoes
result. Impose, furthermore, the pattern of the court of love
(or suggest its imposition) upon the court of Denmark and observe what ironies balefully appear. Claudius rules over a
political court, of course, but Shakespeare alludes—can we
suppose that he does so unintentionally?—by means of the
preoccupation with love shared by the three principal figures
in that court, to matters beyond anything in the sources.
Claudius, the lord of love, Gertrude the queen (or even more
grotesquely, the goddess of love), Hamlet, the youthful devotee of love—it fits as only an intended parody could, a
further example of Shakespeare's modest cunning.

The result is yet another series of balances throughout
the play, similar in effect to the setting off of perfectionist
revenger against reluctant revenger and to the posing of the
revenge motif against the prohibition of revenge, all neatly
dovetailed into the narrative and characterizations, yet at the
same time pulling in utmost tension against one another. To
Hamlet's several roles we add one more, the rebel against
love, the true rebel motivated by the revulsion of the apostate

and not, as in romance, the lighthearted skeptical youth as yet untouched by love's power. For Hamlet has felt and observed the power of love, and it has turned in every instance into cause for loathing. He does not deny love's power, as does the hero of romance before his conversion, saying that it can't happen to him, or that love is a weak emotion of weak men. His is a total revulsion at love's too well known power, for we cannot doubt his earlier romantic and idealized love for Ophelia, to the strength of which he testifies in the graveyard scene.

At first, quite naturally, Hamlet is disgusted, as is the audience, at the spectacle of Claudius and Gertrude enjoying the license of their o'erhasty marriage. This is a travesty of the sweet and dignified obedience to the commandments of love enjoined by the lord and lady of the court of love. The violence of Hamlet's reaction must surprise at first and then lead to further insights on the part of the audience listening to his railing against love and counseling Gertrude and Ophelia to disobey love's commandments. One catches reminiscences of the traditional outcry, inherited from medieval castigators of the daughters of Eve, against all manifestations of profane love.

How, then, is this antiromance, as it might be called, worked into the plot? First, the code of the lover is admirably suited to Hamlet's early determination to play the antic. The distraught lover who appears before Ophelia is so much a part of a familiar pattern, so readily accepted as stage convention that, as revenger, he can use it for a convenient disguise to stalk his intended victim. Not that such disguising takes the audience in, for we have been told that he is pretending. But it is dramaturgically logical that so familiar a convention will deceive the conventional figures on stage—all, that is, save Claudius. Ophelia, Polonius, and Gertrude are all deceived, and it is an indication to the audience of Claudius's astuteness —no mean opponent for Hamlet—that he sees through the ruse. Hamlet's change from pretending melancholy lover, exploiting as disguise the accepted behavior of the code, to genuinely disillusioned railer at the power of lust masquerading as love is another aspect of Hamlet's characterization with which Shakespeare has calculatingly, that is, with modesty and cunning, enlarged his drama far beyond the confines of the revenge play. With these notations in mind, one can more fully appreciate Harbage's description of Hamlet as the most astonishing balancing feat in literature.[4]

Shakespeare's revenge play was not, of course, the only one successfully acted by the King's Men. But no other dramatist really trusted the Globe audience. Marston's *Malcontent* (1604) comes to mind as a prime example of the work of an author so self-consciously and intensely aware of the audience, yet so skeptical of the trustworthiness of its judgment that he panders to what he evidently considers to be the spectators' ingrained self-conscious, proud, vain nature, trying to flatter them with specious intimations of their witty superiority. Hence, in the "Induction" Marston pretends to acknowledge frankly the triteness of a playwright's devices, and, mocking the auditors with this appeal to their amused superiority, seeks actually to disarm criticism. Rather than being invited to participate in the play through moral and emotional involvement, the audience is put at a distance.

Marston presents a travesty of the revenge conventions, seeking to amuse, fascinate, and shock by having his character Malevole exaggerate motives and trickery to the point of becoming a freak, a sideshow figure, a Jonsonian humor character, existing chiefly for the sake of noise and jest. For the Vice character with a Machiavellian vocabulary (which is what Malevole and his numerous disguises amount to) is merely a product of pseudocleverness. Although Marston had considerable talent and experience, his play is about as unsubtle as *The Spanish Tragedy*, which, incidentally, the Children of the Queen's Revels had pirated from the King's Men. In revenge the King's Men, *quid pro quo*, pirated *The Malcontent*, perhaps with Marston's connivance.[5]

These face-to-face encounters with the audience (indulged in by Marston but avoided by Shakespeare) succeed only in making the audience spectators rather than participants. This debarment of the audience was Jonson's fault too, who, because he could not effect Shakespeare's subtle, ironic compounds of traditional materials, boasted that he would not. In his *Every Man in his Humour* he claims to be able to dispense with conventions and to employ language "such as men do use." Nevertheless, his play turns out to be a series of stereotypes, all voluble, all predictable. None of the characters and none of the situations of his dramas, however, make the demands on the audience's informed judgment or sympathy that Shakespeare's plays do. Nor do they confer comparable aesthetic benefits upon the audience.

Except for the character of the Machiavellian villain, Shakespeare makes comparatively little use of the revenge-play conventions after *Hamlet*. Nor does he quite achieve the alloy of conventional types that make a Hamlet, though Iago and Edmund come to mind as other complex amalgams of traditional elements.

The modern mind, preferring the muddier terms of psychology, finds it unenlightened to use words like "evil personified" or "Satanism" to describe Iago. The Elizabethans, however, would not have hesitated to label Iago Satan, deviltry personified, persuaded to this identification early in the play by Iago's obvious inheritances of knavery from the Vice, that ancient associate of Diabolus in the moralities. Iago is even furnished with a set of characteristics reminiscent of the particular Vice Dissimulation, on which are engrafted almost all of the known types of stage reprobate and villain. Are these not the accents of the braggart warrior: "I know my price"? And this the boast of the malcontent, a would-be avenger of fancied slights: "I follow him to serve my turn upon him"? And these the words of the evil counselor: "Reputation is an idle and most false imposition . . ."? The Vice Dissimulation, however, gives significant body and form to Iago's villainy:

> For when my outward action doth demonstrate
> The native act and figure of my heart
> In compliment extern, 'tis not long after
> But I will wear my heart upon my sleeve
> For daws to peck at. I am not what I am.
> [I.i.61–65]

Add to this gift of dissimulation Iago's obvious enjoyment of mischief, another familiar Vice characteristic, and we have, almost, a superfluity of motives ready for any and all occasions, the bilking of Roderigo, for example, or the ruining of Cassio's good name.

Through all of these motives there resounds a note of pride. Iago relishes his skill in dissimulation, his clever phrasing of malcontent sneers at others' idealizing, his deftness in causing mischief, and his fluency in self-confession ("I stand accountant for as great a sin."). Shakespeare of course expects his audience to see the connection between Iago the Vice and Iago the agent of Satan, proud father of all evil, even as earlier audiences had seen the Vice acting to undo mankind in the morality plays. Such discovery alarms the modern mind, however, and it hastens to relegate such notions to footnotes explanatory of Iago's "I am not what I am." Unused to the implication of such phrases, we choose to mull over Iago's references to other motives, as if he were a living person, severely maladjusted to be sure. Not so Shakespeare's audience, who would not have been puzzled by Iago's enjoyment of plotting for its own sake. To spoil Othello's delights, to pretend to be on both sides of a quarrel, to make the whole company drunk and then start a brawl—these are all, perhaps, expected tricks. Unusual, however, would be Iago's finesse in perpetrating them and the occasional hints of a purposefulness to his scheming that his Machiavellian pride suggests. This admixture of purpose to the stereotype Vice would seem novel to the Elizabethans, but not to us. We are, evidently, more at ease with villains whose motives are liable to psychological cataloging.

We have, in part at least, answered already the question of why Shakespeare mixes elements of stereotypes. Nothing succeeds better (or more regularly) in the theater than the familiar to which a degree of novelty is added. In connection with the other question which has guided this inquiry, that is, how does Shakespeare join familiar and novel elements in his plays, we can observe that he uses a quite common stock type or theme and increasingly, in the Globe plays, modifies it.

Thus Iago is patently the Vice to which other ordinarily quite simple characteristics are added. Bernard Spivack, in his *Shakespeare and the Allegory of Evil*,[6] looks at Iago and finds that the Vice characteristics are predominant and at odds with the naturalistic characterizations of the other characters and with the setting and story. This explanation is almost, but not quite, the whole answer to the question of Iago's puzzling and contradictory nature. It is not so much Iago's dramatic environment that creates the tension in the character as it is something within the character himself: the Machiavellian stereotype has been added to the Vice. The Machiavellian mocker of all values rejoices in his sense of his superiority not as an agent of the Evil One but in his own right as being cleverer than other men. This characteristic gives the figure of Iago an ethical coherence absent from the Vice stereotype.

Edmund, although perhaps deficient in one element of the alloy that constitutes Iago, that is, contemptuous hatred of his victims, also inherits from the morality Vice his enjoyment of mischief, which early in the play assumes priority over the "normal" motive of envy of Edgar's legitimacy. "Legitimate Edgar, I must have your lands," an understandable enough motive, pales beside his later "All with me's meet that I can fashion fit." Hence his game of duping Gloucester with "discovered" plots, and his pose as loyal and honest son avenging his father's wrongs seem sport as satisfying to him as the remembrance of sensual joy is pleasurable to Gloucester's unthinking grossness. He is scornful, moreover, of Gloucester's naïve belief in the natural portents of disaster (such scornful mockery being an identifying mark of Shakespeare's villains). But after his success he becomes strangely passive, as if unambitious. Were he like Iago he would of course continue to plot, hate the good and fair and young, and actively try to bring them to ruin. The tenacity of the true Machiavellian is omitted from his character, and he remains a comparatively uncomplicated character, mere agent of evil and not its persistent director as Iago is. There is, consequently, no danger of Edmund's usurping too much attention, as Shylock does, thus upsetting the balance of the plot. He remains in the subplot, appearing only briefly in the main plot, thus not endangering the balanced tension of the twofold tragedy of Lear and Gloucester.

Both Iago and Edmund are villains who would be at home in revenge-play circumstances. In the ambience of tragedy they provide a similar motive force for the action by beginning conflicts, stirring up discord. But they do not end as the revenge-play villain should, for Shakespeare abbreviates their last appearance on stage. An Elizabethan audience might expect a loquaciously defiant-to-the-end or talkatively repentant villain to bring an edifying close to the play. But Shakespeare imposes silence upon Iago. The audience is thus challenged, with Iago's "What you know, you know," to supply an explanation for Iago. The jesting Vice is suddenly turned into an enigma, and any explanation of him apparently demands a reckoning with large issues indeed. For Iago's motives, inherited from traditional characters from whom he is compounded, are generalized evil and mischief. Iago is a particular, individualized agent whose integrity of character as a figure in drama springs from the way in which Shakespeare has him dominate his dramatic environment. He is far from being an exotic personification impossible of accommodation to naturalistic dramatic surroundings. For if he purposefully dominates that dramatic environment, he is certainly related to it and is an integral part of the play's fabric, not a fantastic embroidery upon it.

With Edmund, however, there is preserved something of the repentant villain in his confession that he has ordered the deaths of the imprisoned Lear and Cordelia. Nevertheless, some ambiguity attaches even to this stereotyped behavior. "Some good I mean to do," says Edmund, but how are we to be sure how he means this? Could it not be the last bravado, the final intrusion of himself upon the notice of others so that once again he will be important, not simply the victim of Edgar's righteous sword? Edmund's declaration of good intentions might actually be the cruelest irony, for knowing that his "repentance" is too late to spare his victims he will have doubly triumphed in effecting their deaths and at the same time deceiving others into crediting his claimed repentance.

At any rate, we are compelled to notice Edmund for a time and to remark the discrepancy between his end and the usual adieus of villains. Once again a variation of the stereotype can be seen to be a calculated use of the stereotype.

Revenge themes and revenge-play characters suit well with chronicle, as we have seen. Indeed, the Elizabethan chronicles consist largely of episodes of revenge and counter-revenge. The dramatic conventions of revenge, tragedy, and history are, moreover, in large measure interchangeable. That is, avengers inhabit the chronicle play, and the fall of princes becomes a customary subject of tragedy. Shakespeare combines these elements in *Julius Caesar* and in *Hamlet*. Thereafter, *Lear* and *Macbeth* employ the conventions of the history or state play as framework. *Lear*, for instance, employs the history-play conventions as a quick and expedient way of setting the issues before the audience: the ruler's court, the deficient ruler, the impairment of the crown that presages disaster. At the close, as in *Hamlet*, the nomination of a ruler for the restored state furnishes as tranquil a closing for tragedy as the marriage of true lovers does for romance. As has often been noted, *Lear* has very little rising action, the climax occurring at the very beginning with the result that the hero is apparently more sinned against than sinning. That this apparent defect in the play has nowadays to be analyzed and explained into a real merit is a comment upon our deficiency as much as upon Shakespeare's daring. For Shakespeare took his audience with him in this matter. Instructed in the rudiments of statecraft by the platitudes of chronicle and homily, the people at the Globe knew that the integrity of a kingdom requires that royal power be maintained. To give away a kingdom, to divide it, or to tamper with it in any radical way so as to reduce the power and wholeness of the crown is beyond the competence of a king and is a violation of the interdependent harmony, order, and degree in society, in nature, and in the individual man. Therefore, when Lear gives the crown away, treating it as the symbol of an onerous task rather than of a divinely ordained obligation to maintain the order of nature in his realm, the audience will deem the scale of justice not too unbalanced when Lear thereafter falls so low. For the auditor of 1606, then, Lear's "I am a man more sinned against than sinning" has ironic overtones. He *is* culpable.

It is difficult for us, however, to term Lear's sufferings punishment, for we cannot see his fault in the light cast by the Renaissance notions of history. We are inclined to agree with Lear and cannot discern the magnitude of his sin any more than he could; consequently, we have to make of him (until we read the footnotes) a foolish, irate old man. Shakespeare thus set himself a more difficult task in *Lear* than we can well judge. For after having brought to bear in a moment the whole historical tradition upon the point of Lear's folly, he must in the rest of the play so recount Lear's anguish that the Globe audience will feel sympathy for him in spite of his merited punishment.

Macbeth also has this grounding upon the familiar themes and conventions of the history play and is similarly dignified and enriched by a like employment of the traditional references to the natural correspondences. Far more adept now in their use than when he wrote the history plays, Shakespeare compresses the whole tradition into spectacular imagery of storm and tempest. In the early history plays, such references were merely foreboding (Hal's comments before Shrewsbury), or something imagined by the speaker (Richard II's meditations on his return to England to encounter Bolingbroke). But in the Globe period, the tempest is actually a part of the play's structure. There is, for instance, the irony of the forepassed dangers of the storm in *Othello* before the calm harbor welcomes Desdemona and her lord. In a more intense manner, the images that embody the doctrine of the natural correspondences are concentrated and then explosively released in the tempest preceding Caesar's assassination, a device again employed in *Lear* and in *Macbeth*, wherein, however, the storm becomes on the one hand a projection of the moral nature of the protagonists and, on the other, seems actually to take part in men's affairs far beyond mere sympathy or correspondence.

The storm as projection of character is, of course, seen on

the heath where Lear first rages against his daughters and then answers the storm as if it summoned him to judgment. But this is culmination of much use of the conventional references throughout the play. We are used to hearing the Elizabethans, when they want to be impressive, turn a phrase or two about the correspondences that appear on every hand between the world within man and the world without. Surely the Globe audience could rehearse the scheme *in extenso,* and it would seem that such familiarity, if not at last breeding contempt, would generate merely the inattention accorded ideas and rituals to which we are long used. To build an entire play around such a familiar theme must have seemed to Shakespeare a risky dramatic venture, but (if the audience could be induced to appreciate the convention in its entire and majestic relevance) also a way of imparting the profoundest edification.

The conventional metaphor begins to develop early in the play with Lear's oath by sun, moon, and stars that accompanies his resignation of his crown and rejection of Cordelia. Both human relationships and political decorum are upset and deranged, and Lear becomes a violator of the lawful ordinance of nature and not, save incidentally, the pagan, pre-Christian king, which is often his role in footnotes and articles in learned journals.

In the romantic comedies Shakespeare was fond of presenting a set of time-honored conventions, having them challenged by a skeptic mocker, and then rescuing them intact from this subversion. A similar pattern is evident in *Lear.* Lear's swearing "By all the operation of the orbs / From whom we do exist and cease to be" (I.i.113–14) introduces a metaphorical explanation of man's essence that will be examined by Edmund, who in his analysis of man's relationship to nature cynically rejects Gloucester's interpretation of the meaning of "These late eclipses in the sun and moon." An Elizabethan or Jacobean audience could not help taking sides in this, for it must recognize the portents of disaster in Gloucester's speech as trustworthy statements of tragic foreboding despite the fact that they are contained in the utterances of a man whose good sense and moral probity can be called into question by his gross and cheerfully unrepentant boast of his youthful excesses. On the other hand, such challenges of conventional beliefs as Edmund expresses, however warranted by immediate circumstances, are vitiated by the skeptic's confession of ulterior motives. The alternating affirmation and rejection of the old convention of the relevance of natural phenomena to man's moral nature result in the traditional view remaining finally intact and effective. And when Lear is described as storm-beset humanity who "Strives in his little world of man to out-scorn / The to-and-fro conflicting wind and rain" (III.i.10–11), the contention involves more than the person of the dejected king. For Lear's interpretings of the storm run the gamut of the possible ways of looking at man, his place in nature, and his relationship to the supernatural. Apart from the play these utterances would constitute sententiousness. In this dramatic context, preceded by Edmund's casuistry about nature and by Lear's earlier appeal to the gods of nature, they must profoundly affect our sensibilities. We see, whereas before we merely agreed.

The history-play conventions in *Macbeth*, like those in *Lear*, are easily summarized. The tyrant who outrages the order of the state and rejects the good counselor (Banquo) is destroyed by the supporters of political and social right. It is a framework which encloses the substance of the play. We recognize the familiar history-play decorum when Macbeth, employing the Machiavellian terminologies of a Richard III, sends the murderers, the usual "discontented gentlemen," to waylay Banquo and Fleance. Acceptable lessons in statecraft appear later in Malcolm's subtle dealings with Macduff, thus suggesting Malcolm's qualifications as a shrewd ruler. And the battle in which the avenging armies overwhelm the tyrant is an instructive exhibition, typical of many chronicles, of the meting out of justice.

Amidst all this standard fare, however, Macbeth's character is at once dignified and shaped by the natural correspondences. The sergeant's narration to Duncan of Macbeth's battle against the traitorous Cawdor, for example, is replete with old-fashioned references to portents and natural sympathies:

As whence the sun 'gins his reflection
Shipwrecking storms and direful thunders break,
So from that spring whence comfort seem'd to come,
Discomfort swells.

[I.ii.25–28]

Again, there are the speculations of Lennox, Ross, and the Old
Man on the implications of the direfully portentous night of
storm and tempest. Gathering strength from these familiar
notes, recognizable to the audience and acceptable as a traditional theme, there develop a strangeness and power. Nature,
rather than being correspondent to men's affairs, becomes an
active interferer. For the doctrine that the order of nature can
be only temporarily disrupted by tempests seems to be denied.
Macbeth himself becomes spokesman for this total negation
of all power of goodness as he meditates:

Now o'er the one half-world
Nature seems dead, and wicked dreams abuse
The curtain'd sleep. Now witchcraft celebrates
Pale Hecate's offerings.

[II.i.49–52]

Nature itself has divisions, and these affect man through man's
willingness to enlist on one side or the other of the conflict.
Ambiguities such as had never been ascribed to the doctrine
of correspondences in any other play are introduced. For the
witches' relationship to nature is itself ambiguous. They seem
sometimes to be allied with nature, possessing some kind of
control, as if they were aspects of nature yet at war with
nature's order. They control the elements for their malevolent
purposes: "I'll give thee a wind." "And I another." "I myself
have all the other." But their malevolence can take effect only
through their human instrument Macbeth, whom they, paradoxically, delight in bringing to a ruin which in turn deprives
them of the agent of their power, that is, Macbeth himself.
Thus we have a wrenching of the conventional theme: the
order of nature, rather than merely reflecting and sympathiz-
ing with men's tragic deeds, as in most other plays, seems

finally to restore itself to wholeness and is once again reflected in the ordered state ensured by Malcolm's victory. Shakespeare takes, once more, the familiar convention, reverses it, and then restores it. But by emphasizing it beyond the other conventions in the play, he makes the final restoration of conventional order take on added significance. The play thus achieves its full moral intensity which, perhaps, can be phrased as a denial of the power of evil to do more than temporarily disrupt the orderly processes of nature, not only in the world outside man but in man himself. Without the antecedent familiar convention, however, this final meaning would be impossible.

The metaphor that pictures the world of man and the world of nature as mutually reflecting images dignifies and enlarges themes and characters. So it is with *Lear* and *Macbeth*, both of which to be sure have themes of weight and moment in the edificatory tradition of "true chronicle" history. But *Othello*, only slightly involved in this tradition as far as its narrative is concerned, also draws upon the metaphor of nature to dignify the hero. Othello's imagination, ranging beyond the confines of Cyprus and Venice, invokes the attention of all nature to his disaster:

> Methinks it should be now a huge eclipse
> Of sun and moon, and that th' affrighted globe
> Should yawn at alteration.
>
> [V.ii.99–101]

What is essentially a domestic tragedy becomes generalized morality. In no other way could an Elizabethan writer dignify his narrative; in no other way would an Elizabethan audience have assented to the elevation of a tale of jealousy and deception, of deceived husband and wronged wife, to tragic importance. Shakespeare alone among his fellow playwrights succeeds in thus exalting such a story above the merely pathetic (Heywood's *Woman Killed with Kindness*, for example) or the grossly sensational *(The Yorkshire Tragedy)*.

Othello is reminiscent of *Romeo and Juliet* in this use of metaphors of nature to lend dignity to the hero. Romeo speaks of the stars and sea and storm that circumscribe his woeful history, and Othello speaks of voyages through storm-beset seas to a destination that proves not the haven he expected. They are furthermore alike in idealizing love. Romeo was true to the code of honorable love, save for his tragic momentary lapse of placing honor and revenge above love when he slew Tybalt. But Othello, in seconding Desdemona's request to the Venetian senators to be allowed to accompany him to Cyprus, professed himself not wholly bound by the tenets of romantic love (I.iii.268–71). His character, therefore, in terms of the well-known interpretations of love's honorable bondage, would be regarded as liable to flaw and error. To place his service to the state above his love; to say "My life upon her faith" without adding "and her life upon my faith," in short not swearing to consecrate his honor to her service—these were surely forebodings of tragedy.

Thus it is that Shakespeare even in the midst of composing tragedy increasingly relies upon the conventions of romantic love. They appear everywhere (in what to the modern observer must seem the most unlikely places) and are productive of unexpected conclusions about fate and character. For in the tragedies a touch or two of the love conventions can identify hero or villain, can reveal clearly the depth of Iago's villainy, and in a moment distinguish between the morally sound and the morally diseased. Regan and Goneril, for example, twist and distort the conventional relationships of love into a grotesque parody, making Edmund their prey. Goneril's language hints of the convention, for instance, when she "commands" Edmund to prove himself worthy of her favor:

> Ere long you are like to hear,
> If you dare venture in your own behalf
> A mistress' commands
>
> [IV.ii.19–21]

To which Edmund responds with a pat bit of bravado straight from the code of the chivalric observance of the lady's absolute power over her lover: "Yours in the ranks of death."

Iago, however, stands as the foremost example of Shake-

speare's reliance upon the courtly code to fashion, paradoxically, the consummate villain. At first conventional mocker at
love—or so he seems—he sneers at Roderigo's playing the role
of foolish lover who desperately cons all the rules of love and
woefully misapplies them. Duping Roderigo is, however,
child's play for Iago. But it is ironically appropriate that
Roderigo is the only one whom Iago openly tries to convert to
his way of thinking by couching his arguments in terms used
by the would-be villains of romance, who would applaud his
cynical identification of love and lust.

Not that Iago cannot understand the force of the conventional belief in the restorative power of love. He does; and he
shows considerable knowledge of the tradition in using others'
faith in it to gain control over them. It is not the fool whom
Iago hates; it is the man of gentle and noble heart. And how
shall this gentle and noble man be better identified than by his
commitment (in terms of the Renaissance literary tradition)
to the ideals of love and honor couched in the metaphors of
the religion of love? These phrases and the faith prefigured in
them infuriate Iago. And it is in his reaction to these phrases
that Iago's Satanism can be best descried. Desdemona describes her love as a consecration. Iago mocks such profession
of faith as "sanctimony and a frail vow." Cassio is extrava-
gantly addicted to the forms of worship of fair ladies decreed
by the courtly tradition as he welcomes Desdemona to
Cyprus:

> Ye men of Cyprus, let her have your knees.
> Hail to thee, lady! and the grace of heaven,
> Before, behind thee, and on every hand
> Enwheel thee round!
>
> [II.i.84–87]

Iago immediately marks him for another victim, an angelic
figure, like Desdemona, whose brightness makes Iago ugly in
his own eyes. But Iago never plays the condemner of love in
their presence. He seems to realize that his machinations can
never alter Desdemona's love, nor corrupt the veneration accorded her by Cassio.

Iago is left with only Othello as instrument whereby he can attack and subvert this religion of love and all that it, metaphorically, stands for. What makes Othello susceptible is the inadequate and incomplete union of love and honor that renders him liable to the sin of suspicious pride, surely a familiar note in Renaissance literature. Othello has, as we have noted, saved a part of his nature from the domination of love:

> When light-wing'd toys
> Of feather'd Cupid seel with wanton dullness
> My speculative and offic'd instruments,
>
> [I.iii.268–71]

he will not be a great commander. He means this, in part, as a jest appropriate at the time of speaking. But it is actually an ironic presage of disaster, no less significant than his turning to Iago with the epithet "honest."

As the narrative progresses, the principal characters repeatedly have their roles as well as their moral dispositions defined according to the traditional religion of love. Cassio's welcoming metaphor in Cyprus clearly assigns Desdemona the role of goddess of love. Othello speaks movingly of the garden of true being:

> But there where I have garner'd up my heart,
> Where either I must live or bear no life,
> The fountain from the which my current runs,
> Or else dries up—to be discarded thence.
>
> [IV.ii.57–60]

He is, nevertheless, guilty of the primal sin of pride. Proud of his honor and his reputation, he is tempted by Iago and falls into disbelief, having been persuaded that at last he knows good and evil. It is fitting, moreover, that Iago refer to himself in epithets suggestive of treachery—as a Turkish infidel if, as he says, he does not speak the truth: "or else I am a Turk," meaning, of course, that he no more tells the truth than does any unbelieving enemy of the true faith. These repeated references to the religion-of-love tradition render, in effect, the metaphor of the religion of love both control and focus of the play.

Lest all of this seem merely an attempt at subtilization to the point where logic vanishes, we must recall Shakespeare's long-continued use of the religion-of-love metaphor and how often it has served him well. It seems then not too farfetched to suppose that by the time he writes *Othello* it has become natural for him to think of characters and motives in terms of that metaphor. From it and its conventional expressions he has suggested most powerfully the connections between the actuality of life, which the drama purports to be, and the conflict of abstract moral forces of which religion and philosophy speak.

No other Elizabethan dramatist was able to do this. Jonson, for example, never pushes the limits of drama so far. His subversive characters, knaves and cheats, are never caught up in such hatred; they are not concerned with destroying ideals. They scorn their victims, but unlike Iago, do not hate them. The conventions Jonson works with do not admit of the metaphorical extension required by great tragedy. Webster and Ford sometimes achieve the full expression of passion, but they lack the skill to fashion a play like *Othello* from conventions (the natural correspondences and the code of revenge) that yield ironic overtones when juxtaposed to so flexibly evocative a metaphor as the religion of love with its conventional forms of speech, motive, even stereotyped characters. So much evidence abounds of Shakespeare's mature skill in this that one could long continue spelling out details. It is better to conclude with citing the most affecting use of the religion of love to enlarge the scope of tragedy: the grotesque and dehumanizing parody of the courtly code by Goneril and Regan, a parody that renders apt Lear's diatribe against love as he sees the blinded Gloucester: "Dost thou squiny at me? No, do thy worst, blind Cupid; I'll not love" (IV.vi.140–41).

Other dramatists attempted to adapt the romanticization of history, popular in ballad and prose narrative, to the stage. These attempts, however, even the most nearly successful ones, Greene's for example in *James IV* and *Friar Bacon*, or

Marlowe's in *Tamburlaine*, are marred by an excessive and naïve use of the romance conventions. In his history plays, Shakespeare avoids extravagant imposition of courtly conventions upon historical narrative. The religion-of-love conventions, for example, though often an essential part of the dramatic structure of his tragedies, are more often than not merely incidental in the history plays. *Richard III* saw the conventions exploited by the Machiavellian in one brilliant scene; Percy was an uncouth courtier; Henry V enjoyed himself as a mock-serious wooer. But with *Antony and Cleopatra* Shakespeare seems bent on a full-scale romanticization of history that results in the elevation of history, or the "state play," to the level of tragedy. The account he drew upon in Plutarch's *Lives* is principally history. His selection of incident from Plutarch, however, serves to set in opposition the idealization of courtly love and the conventions of the state play. The final issue generated by this set of tensions, if we may call them so, is the simultaneous defeat and victory, or victory in defeat, of the romantic ideal. Octavius, like Iago, believes that he has to corrupt and destroy his enemies' ideals, not just their persons; and his chief strategy, again like Iago, is to have the idealists betray their own faith. His motive, however, since this is a history play, is the more readily understood one of preserving the security of the state, whereas Iago has, in terms of merely "human nature," only cynical malevolence as his temporal spur.

The old romantic faith is endangered by this onslaught of Octavius's world of empire and power. But it is equally imperiled by the initial weakness and folly of the devotees themselves. Indeed, it seems as if Shakespeare were trying to make it impossible for love to triumph. For he shows up in all their artificial frailty the conventional poses, language, and roles of the courtly tradition until toward the end of the play when those who conducted their lives, however imperfectly, according to the tenets of the code choose fidelity to the old faith.

The conventions are initially subjected to some severe strains by the hero and heroine, the audience being asked to listen to repeated near betrayals of the doctrine—close to the

mood of Beaumont and Fletcher in their tragicomedies. For
instance, the very fact of Antony's age and his too experienced
command of the language of love render his protestations
suspect as, with a flourish, he bids farewell to Cleopatra:

> By the fire
> That quickens Nilus' slime, I go from hence
> Thy soldier, servant, making peace or war
> As thou affect'st.
>
> [I.iii.68–71]

No hero of chivalric romance could speak more correctly or
use the conventional epithet "servant" more deftly. Thus it is
with all of the courtly phrases. They take on ironic meanings,
poignancy sometimes, when men and women experienced in
the art of love speak them. The conventions seem out of context, as we can tell from our having first seen them in romances
acted out by heroes and heroines expressing their first, fresh
love. Nevertheless, when Antony attempts to break the "strong
Egyptian fetters," he raises the same question of the primacy
of love or honor and their possible harmonization that occu-
pied the courts of love in medieval romance, where debates
were often enlivened by citation of his fidelity to Cleopatra,
herself triumphantly installed in a place of eminence as one
of the martyrs of love in the *Legend of Good Women*.

Cleopatra's dilemma, like Antony's, is fashioned for the
most part of the contentions possible within the framework of
the courtly code. She, however, tends to oversubtilize the role
decreed for the lady in the love game and instead of employing the simple, direct command over her lover, given her by
the code, becomes too clever. Again, this is the result of too
much experience. We hear sufficient warnings, for instance,
when Charmian cautions against too much crossing of Antony.
This school-of-love precept is rejected forthrightly by Cleopatra: "Thou teachest like a fool." Such exchanges, however,
by defining Cleopatra's character and making her motives dramatically credible, enable us to admit as legitimately part of
the narrative the wildest exaggeration possible to the courtly
tradition, that is, to have the hero literally give up the world
for love—as Antony does at Actium.

One would be hard put to it to name the primary theme of *Antony and Cleopatra*, so entwined are the traditions of romance and history and so numerous the uses of conventions, often merely suggested in shorthand fashion. The sensitivity of Shakespeare's audience to all of these, however, made it possible for him to assimilate many of the conventions in this romantic tragedy. Connoisseurs of romance, and all early seventeenth-century audiences were such, would admire the astuteness with which the courtly tradition is preserved intact at the end of the play. The political theorists in the audience, and all seventeenth-century Englishmen were such, would perforce be drawn into active speculation about Octavius's motives and enjoy the way in which they can recognize the Machiavellian adept who exploits his enemies' weaknesses but acts in the service of the grand Roman ideal of universal empire and universal peace. Next to *Hamlet, Antony and Cleopatra* is probably the most complex of Shakespeare's plays and another magnificent balancing act.

Two plays of this Globe period stand out as different from the others: *Coriolanus,* because it lacks the intermingling of traditions that gives vitality to the other tragedies, and *Troilus and Cressida,* because it tries but fails to intermingle traditions. *Coriolanus* is a nonalloyed play, so to speak, compounded almost wholly of edificatory conventions of the history-play tradition with the result that it seems, in comparison with Shakespeare's other Roman plays, narrowly confined in theme and imagery.

The political theme is stated at the very beginning, more explicitly than in any other play except for Ulysses' speech in *Troilus and Cressida,* conveying edification pure and simple not only to the Roman plebeians on stage but to the English subjects of King James in the audience. The play's conventional references are strung together to make a craftsmanlike job, and such dramatic tension as the play contains results chiefly, it seems, from Shakespeare's having his characters play their roles of assent or dissent against a background of familiar doctrine.

Coriolanus assents to the doctrine, but like an indiscriminately ardent supporter, actually undermines it in practice.

When he lectures the tribunes, for example, he speaks aristocratic orthodoxy: the people shall not judge, for their fickle-
ness and ignorance render them politically incapable as well
as militarily unreliable. This official and acceptable doctrine
takes on ironic overtones when put into the mouth of one
whose motivation is not solicitude for those whom he must
govern but scorn and contempt. For the misinstructed ruler
who, like Coriolanus, knows only the form of order but not its
spirit brings disaster to the state.

   Coriolanus is an extraordinary play for its time, and quite
exceptional in the Shakespeare canon. This special quality results largely from the absence of either conflict of conventions
or synthesis of conventions. Conventions of romance do not
appear, even for occasional motivations; nor do the natural
correspondences appear in the expected form of portents fore-
shadowing disasters to the state. The play seems, consequently, barren and unenriched, and Coriolanus himself
brittle, the least poetically minded, hence the least amiable
of Shakespeare's heroes. These qualities have, to be sure, been
recommendations of the play to some modern Shakespeareans
who relish its bleakness.

   Coriolanus, a grimly simple play, found some favor
among the audience at the Globe; but *Troilus and Cressida*,
an ornate play, apparently none. Yet it is full of the conventional touches that would ordinarily ensure success. Shakespeare apparently wrote it not for the Globe audience but for
a special one, probably the young wits from the Inns of
Court.[7] Working without the guidance of what he knew were
the expectations of the public audience, he seems to be unde-
cided as to his goal. The Globe audience, evidently, liked to
have the conventions of romance and history, after temporary
paradox and questioning, emerge intact in form and theme.
But in *Troilus and Cressida* this does not happen. Too much
strain is put upon the traditions; the synthesis and balance that
might produce effective drama are not attained, and the result is not a structured drama but a pile of fragments, many
of them glittering, to be sure, but without true formal connection with each other.

The political theme of the play is taken quite seriously—
at first. Ulysses' speech on order and degree is one that a brilliant aspirant to the dignity of crown counsel would admire.
But even Ulysses, at first a serious spokesman for received
opinions, proves an enjoyer of buffoonery as he encourages
Ajax in rivalry with Achilles. And thus it is throughout the
play. A conventional character, theme, or situation is no sooner
presented than it is made ridiculous. Ulysses exercises himself
to kindle the cause of honor in Achilles' breast—and to awaken
in the audience's mind the expectation of participating according to custom in a contention between honor and love. But the
promised contention never materializes; it is turned into mockery of the romantic convention that requires the hero to sac-
rifice even his honor at the lady's behest when, instead of making a proud declaration of loyalty to love, Achilles winces as
Ulysses reveals that he knows of Achilles' pledge to the Trojan
princess to refrain from battle. Achilles' secret love for Polyxena being thus treated as a wretched little secret, the conventional romantic plot and characterizations are caricatured.
The play itself, after the scene of Achilles' failure to live up to
the stature of romantic hero, wanders from episode to episode,
no more successful in developing romance or even antiromance from the love of Troilus and Cressida than from
Achilles' woes. For Troilus, even as Achilles, is a failure as
hero of a romantic tragedy. Too much is made of Troilus's dis-
illusionment; there is, on the one hand, too much of serious and
eloquent protestations of love and, on the other, too little of
faith in love. Since the play's romantic conventions have little
connection with the history-play conventions (never being
brought into conflict) the play becomes a hodgepodge of cleverness merely.

From the earliest of the Globe plays in 1599 to those toward
the end the first decade of the seventeenth century, there is
almost everywhere a high level of technical proficiency. The
familiar and modestly introduced conventions are, by juxtapo-
sition, opposition and combination, developed into effective
devices of dramatic structure. The conventions are neither

rejected nor transformed; their moral content, moreover, remains the same. The traditions, both literary and ethical, are confirmed. Shakespeare seeks not for a new world, nor does he create a new soul for the age. It is the old world, the familiar one made wonderfully real and splendid. Throughout the Globe period, however, the conventions most useful to Shakespeare's dramaturgy prove increasingly to be those of romance. He turns to them for enrichments of tragedy and of history. In the period of reflection that follows *Coriolanus*, the conventions of romance become his sole reliance, as if they, better than any other, embodied for him the soul of the age.

VI

The Last Plays:
A Quality of Strangeness

"There is," said Bacon, "no excellent beauty that hath not some strangeness in the proportion." This is true in a way of all of Shakespeare's plays that we have been considering; for to familiar convention there has been added a countering unfamiliarity. An astringent quality thus results from the calculated admixture of the customary and the novel. At first glance, however, the last plays appear to be altogether strange, their locale wholly exotic, their action occurring in a timeless world, and their themes completely fanciful—an overabundance of the qulaity of strangeness, hence a defect of true excellence. And so it would be were it not for certain conventional ingredients which, by affording a persistent reminder of familiarity, enhance the quality of strange yet excellent beauty.

Shakespeare's drama is marked by the perdurance of the romance conventions, especially those of courtly romance, which find a place even in tragedy and history. As if he were consciously working toward a summary of his art, Shakespeare in these last plays selects the conventions from which he can fashion the best play of which he is capable and in which he can incorporate the ideas to which he is most genuinely committed. Of these conventions the one he principally settles on is the religion of love as the most adaptable to stage narrative and the most expressive of his own and his audience's moral tenets. It is taken more seriously than ever before and ex-

ploited more thoroughly. The plays based upon it are, however, far more than expositions of moral virtue. For the metaphors of the religion of love have the dual virtue of serving at
once as vehicles of ethical instruction when characters affirm
their loyalty to the old faith and as sources of dramatic conflict
when the tenets of romantic love are attacked by jealous
incredulity and suspicion as in *Cymbeline* and *The Winter's
Tale*.

After the triumphs of the Globe period, Shakespeare
makes a new start with *Cymbeline* (1609). That he should return to such naïve romance after the sophistication of *Antony
and Cleopatra* hints at a deliberate choice. For he incorporates
the veriest clichés of plot and character: the long-lost sons of
royal Cymbeline, the parting of lovers by the threats of a
tyrannical father, the reunion of parent and child, the happy
encounter of youth and maid.

In its religion-of-love theme, however, *Cymbeline* is in a
way a retelling of *Othello*. Iachimo's motives at times resemble Iago's; he too wants to discredit and destroy faith in idealized love. Like Othello, Posthumus, feeling himself betrayed,
believes that his sacred honor can be preserved only through
accomplishing the death of the false lady. Posthumus and
Iachimo are, however, more simply than Othello and Iago, the
reshaping of figures of the tradition that from medieval times
on proclaimed love of man and woman a worthy parallel to
religious love and subversions of the faith of lovers, the chief
aim of evildoers.

As if to make Posthumus's betrayal of Imogen the more
shocking, Shakespeare endows her with all the attractiveness
of his earlier heroines. Wit, charm, grace, all exhibited in
especially light and clever handling of the conventional love-
game comedy language, are hers. Hear her, for example, play
with the religion-of-love metaphor, exaggerating it prettily,
mocking it from time to time, rendering it more expressive of
true love than perfervid declarations. As she thinks of Posthumus journeying to Italy, she speaks in phrases that
Chrétien's humorless heroines would have envied, for the faith
is the same:

> Or I could make him swear
> The shes of Italy should not betray
> Mine interest and his honor; or have charg'd him
> At the sixth hour of morn, at noon, at midnight,
> T'encounter me with orisons, for then
> I am in heaven for him.
>
>   [I.iii.26–31]

The religion-of-love convention necessarily invites heretical differences—an excellence, dramatically speaking, from which Shakespeare has often profited. Thus Imogen's outcry on finding Posthumus's cruel letters:

> The scriptures of the loyal Leonatus
> All turn'd to heresy. Away, away,
> Corrupters of my faith!
>
>   [III.iv.83–85]

Ironically, Imogen's coreligionist, Posthumus, has turned corrupt heretic at the promptings of his too trusting sense of honor, which in turn leads to his tragic division of commitment, a fatal separation of love and honor. For Posthumus makes his cause the defense of abstract honor, his own and his lady's, and thus arouses the cynicism of those realists (on stage as well as in the audience) who would not mind boasts about the lady's beauty—opinion merely and therefore not alarming or challenging—but who find the religion-of-love metaphor offensive because it expresses seriously a faith in the substance of things hoped for. The belief that ideals such as faithful love and unassailable chastity exist objectively is a matter for spiteful jesting and vicious mockery by all Iachimos and Iagos, and they must—it is their dramatic function—attempt not only to ensnare the idolator but to destroy the idolatry itself. But "idolatry" cannot be destroyed save by corrupting the faith, not just the person, of the true believer. And this, Iachimo, like Iago, sets out to do. Unlike Iago, however, he schemes and plots not in a "real" sixteenth-century Venice and Cyprus, but in a strange modern Italy that is also imperial Rome and in a Britain that is ally of imperial Caesar as well as modern inheritor of the imperial vogue, a second Rome. It is a world in which time is so fantastically arranged that it becomes timeless, a world colored by the religion-of-love metaphor, an age of faith which the atheist Iachimo believes he can shake at his own will.

Iachimo presents himself as a well-known type, more fully exposed than any such since Shakespeare's early comedies. He knows the rules of the school of love, has mastered all of its tricks of language and suggestions, and has command of its literature. His first move against Imogen at Cymbeline's court is to test her susceptibility to the frailties traditionally ascribed to those unworthy of love and, more searchingly, to tempt her to revenge herself for Posthumus's infidelities fabricated by Iachimo in the hope that she will jealously believe.

The school of love as usual offers lessons for the foolish lover as well as for the honest youth. Cloten, fashioned in Shakespeare's usual way from several stereotypes (braggart, rustic clown, inept wooer), is at once a parody of the gentlemanly lover and, most curiously, of the villain: he is a distorted mirroring of both Posthumus and Iachimo. In all but his taste for music, he is clownish. But "Hark, Hark the Lark," the aubade Cloten causes to be sung for Imogen, we must suppose to be taken as both seriousness and mockery, as a lyric admirably suited to the Lady Imogen and deplorably inappropriate to the clownish wooer Cloten.

The complexities of the love game, despite the queen's earnest coaching, are too deep for Cloten. The involved arguments, pledges asked for but not given, suits and pleas rejected, all make him feel that his honor has somehow been outraged. Like Posthumus, he seeks revenge. Fool and hero are thus caught in the same dilemma, but Posthumus does not have the excuse of doltishness for his behavior. Once more, as in the early comedies, the foolish lover's antics excite the scorn that the audience might otherwise feel for courtly romance unrelieved by comedy.

In *Cymbeline,* Shakespeare uses almost everything that came to hand for a dramatist of his time and experience. Some scenes, indeed, are hard to account for except as arbitrary inclusions of edificatory spectacle intended to teach, as both myth and romance do, that there is a supernatural ordering of men's lives for the good. Posthumus's vision, for example, in which parents and brothers intercede with Jupiter in Posthumus's behalf, impels romance to its proper goal, the revelation of the instructive harmony of love and honor. We have believed that much is cruel chance in a universe where Jupiter has been inattentive. We learn finally that Jupiter has observed and noted all, that he rules well throughout his universal domain.

The court where judgments are formulated and imposed, always expected, always approved as a closing scene, was the normal setting for the dispensing of poetic justice, whether in history, tragedy, or romance. Especially appropriate in *Cymbeline*, it serves as fitting milieu for the blending of romance and history, with this reservation, however: to preserve the spirit of romance the true villains will have to meet their due punishment well beforehand lest their deserved deaths seem the chief cause of the rejoicing of the meritorious. The screams from the dungeon must not, in romance, mingle with the festive notes of reunited families and lovers. Such an embarrassment is delicately avoided in *Cymbeline* by getting rid of Cloten and the queen well in advance of the final scene (though their deaths evidently persuaded the Folio editors to classify the play as tragedy rather than comedy), and Cymbeline merely remembers the queen's death as good riddance of a wicked counselor. Nevertheless, in this last scene Cymbeline flares up repeatedly, a minister of justice inclined to judge prematurely and wrathfully. But as the scene progresses, general forgiveness becomes the mood, and we sense that more is intended than the usual conveniently cheerful ending. The convention is being packed with overtones. Something moves behind the surface appearance of the old tradition in such phrases as Posthumus's words to Iachimo, that repentant heretic in the religion of love:

> The pow'r that I have on you is to spare you;
> The malice towards you to forgive you.
> [V.v.418-19]

Thus, Jupiter's ordering of events bears fruit in a conclusion arranged for and desired by the divine power.

The reconciliation extends to Rome and Britain, to history itself. In the soothsayer's words, the eagle flying westward shows that

> The imperial Caesar should again unite
> His favor with the radiant Cymbeline,
> Which shines here in the West.
>   [V.v.474–76]

Here is a metaphor for the seventeenth-century mind to conjure with. Britain inherits the splendor of Rome and compounds with it her own vigor. Britain is the Rome of King James's time. A text like "Britain is Rome restored" would appeal to every schoolboy and educated Englishman, and is admirably suited to pageant and masque. But if it is to prevail in the theater, it must become adjunct to some narrative, a conventional romance, say, like that of Imogen and Posthumus, devotees in the religion of love. By interweaving it with romance, Shakespeare has made it sound drama, something that Greene never succeeded in achieving, for romance allows the use of coincidence that, in Shakespeare's usage, at last reveals the operation of some guiding force not only upon individual lives but upon the very being of the state, as is implied by Cymbeline's "Heaven mend all."

If *Cymbeline* is a final romanticization of history, *The Winter's Tale* may be regarded as the final romanticization of revenge tragedy. Bound at first by the conventions of revenge, the hero frees himself, and all other characters, by the unqualified acceptance of the dictates of the religion of love. This is a sketchy enough plot resumé, but one which will stand up under examination

Early in the play, the audience is given to understand that the plot is a familiar imbroglio: the honorable friendship of Leontes and Polixenes is threatened by Leontes' dishonorable, jealous suspicion. Like a revenge-play hero he searches for a cause and interprets all evidence in light of his own belief that his honor has been besmirched. He then fancies himself free to plot, threaten, devise punishments, ensnare his enemies, all in the name of his cherished honor. The means employed to narrate Leontes' search for revenge are the well-tried conventions of the love game, an aspect of the play whose significance is often overlooked. Leontes, by judgments deficient in appreciation of the courtly code of love, must appear a jealous lunatic. But his aberration really does have some rational foundation. His derangement springs not from a deterioration of the mind but from a malfunction of the moral sense, an illness, in short, which can be cured by moral amendment. For to Leontes and to Shakespeare's audience Polixenes' opening words must seem an extraordinarily significant way of drawing attention to the queen's advanced pregnancy:

> Nine changes of the watery star have been
> The shepherd's note since we have left our throne
> Without a burden.

> [I.ii.1–3]

The evident fruits of love and the presence of the guest king, thus strongly associated, give Leontes something to notice. He is, furthermore, rational enough in deducing his suspicions from the evidence of familiar conventions of romantic love. He rehearses, for instance (I.ii.284–89), the code of the lover and the lessons of the school of love, and, because he has observed one action included in that code, assumes, logically enough when such codes decree patterned behavior, the acting of the whole. "Stopping the career of laughter with a sigh" then functions as a synecdoche. It is warrant that the entire code, which in old-fashioned parlance asserted the freedom of love from the restrictions of marriage bonds by urging clandestine and adulterous love, has been acted out.

This unsettled and perilous state of affairs (familiar to viewers of tragedy and romance as sure harbinger of disaster) is contrasted with the orderliness that should prevail in an apt sequence in the very center of the play. Cleomenes and Dion, in the first scene of act III, marvel at the delicate climate and celestially garbed inhabitants of the island of the temple of Apollo. They speak as sojourners in a more orderly world and now bring with them the oracle as a prescription of truth from the god of that realm of ordered nature and man.

This scene immediately follows the one in which Leontes, seeking revenge, orders Antigonus to take the child and expose it "where chance may nurse or end it." This "revenge" is an alteration of the convention which speaks of such losses of innocent child and kindred as accidental and unsought for. This deliberate incurring of loss perhaps attracted Shakespeare to Greene's story *Pandosto*. For it suggests the paradox of the fortunate fall of the hero, necessarily antecedent to his redemption, a sequence far more dramatically stimulating than the mere coincidence of romantic happenstance.

Tragedy is thus countered, and revenge purged, by the addition of purpose that corrects the aimless, episodic quality of romance. As a result, the answers to the questions upon which the plot turns transcend both tragedy and revenge: What happens if love's goddess, presumed false, be found true? What penance is adequate for the willful sinner against love? What enshrinement is suitable for love's martyred queen? Such questions are appropriate to romance only and require answers obtainable only by employing romantic conventions to unravel the plot.

As if in preparation for the answers to these ponderings, the pretty conventions of the love game are rehearsed. Florizel courts Perdita, for example, in a school of love. The disguised Polixenes, posing as a connoisseur of the art of wooing, demands of his son some proof of his skill in courtship: "But to your protestation; let me hear what you profess" (IV.iv.379–80). To which Florizel responds with as extravagant a statement of commitment to love's service as any hero of the early comedies:

> Were I the fairest youth
> That ever made eye swerve, had force and knowledge
> More than was ever man's, I would not prize them
> Without her love; for her employ them all;
> Commend them and condemn them to her service
> Or to their own perdition.
>
> [IV.iv.384–89]

Perdita is altogether a heroine of pastoral romance. Resolutely so, one might add, for Shakespeare goes out of his way to keep her true conventional character uncontaminated. She refuses to divert romance from its proper end of resolving all difficulties within its own world. She does not, like the heroines of bourgeois romance, become a warrior for the rights of the humble and middle class to engage in romantic love. That life is good in cottage and in palace she acknowledges, but she does not quarrel about it:

> I was not much afeard; for once or twice
> I was about to speak, and tell him plainly
> The self-same sun that shines upon his court
> Hides not his visage from our cottage, but
> Looks on all alike.
>
> [IV.iv.453-57]

Imagine what havoc it would make of this romance if Perdita were insisted upon as truly a shepherd's daughter whose merit shone in her proud assurance that her love was as good as that of any princess.

The faith that wins over all obstacles, in this play as in Shakespeare's best romances, is embodied in the religion of love. Those who see Perdita cannot help using the familiar metaphors, as the courtier does when he describes her:

> This is a creature,
> Would she begin a sect, might quench the zeal
> Of all professors else; make proselytes
> Of who she but bid follow.
>
> [V.i.106-9]

Thus does Shakespeare prepare for the fullest, most direct, and most obvious use of the religion-of-love metaphor, more complete and pure than even in the early comedies, where, many assume, he is at his most conventional. For in the last scene of *The Winter's Tale* metaphor itself is acted out, not used as a figure of speech merely. Paulina challenges Leontes' faith: If his belief is sound, she promises, the "statue" of Hermione will give some sign of life. The goddess of love will assume life. "It is required you do awake your faith." Leontes' awakened faith, then, brings to conclusion this strangely excellent permeation of the religion-of-love metaphor with a suggested belief in the objective existence of beauty, love, and honor, a faith that, Shakespeare implies (and finds it dramatically possible and desirable to say), finds its only true medium in romantic drama.

It is one of the ironies of Shakespearean criticism that *The Tempest*, one of the most conventional of his plays, is often termed his most original, a work of untrammeled genius, whereas the early plays *Two Gentleman* and *Comedy of Errors*, in which Shakespeare is learning to combine different conventions into one dramatic continuum are blamed for being conventionally derivative. Actually, *The Tempest* is so perfectly conventional that it ends by being a harmonization of those conventions which Shakespeare has found most serviceable; and it is in this respect, as well as in theme, imagery, and handling of verse, a summation of what he felt he could do and wanted to do in drama.

In respect of derivation from sources, however, *TheTempest* is quite original with Shakespeare, for such sources as have been suggested are naïve accounts of voyages to the new world and artless narratives of exiled ruler and child returning to a rightful inheritance. Therefore, it is said, Shakespeare works pretty much with a free hand, disembarrassed of obligation to a particular chronicle. He is free to think his own thoughts. All of this is true and needs to be supplemented only by the reminder that Shakespeare thinking is Shakespeare phrasing his thoughts in the patterns of stage and literary conventions. Thus, we discover him emphasizing his two favorite sets of conventions, the natural correspondences and the religion of love.

In structure the play is of the simplest, as if Shakespeare were reaching back to his apprenticeship for the elementary devices that served in *The Comedy of Errors*, for example, or in *The Taming of the Shrew;* that is, the strictures of the classic farce upon time and place and character types. There are, for example, the scheming servant and tyrannical father to keep the intrigue going. To these are added a story of usurpation avenged and a tale of wooing, prettily sketched and briefly told.

Ariel's role, despite the fanciful attributes of spirit substance, is indeed (even as Puck's was) that of *servus*, as he dashes hither and thither on his master's ceaseless errands. He manages some things himself, however, and enjoys playing tricks of his own devising on the shipwrecked crew and passengers. But, typical of Shakespeare's mature practice, the scope of the convention is strangely enlarged when Ariel's language assumes wider references and intimations. When chastising and correcting the "three men of sin," Alonso, Sebastian, and Antonio, he speaks like an agent of a supernatural power: "I and my fellows / Are ministers of fate" (III.iii.60–61).

Similarly compressed are the conventional history-play references: Alonso, surrounded by evil counselors; envy urging the usurper to strike; the ideal commonwealth pictured in Gonzalo's rambling address. Even the implicit edification in the story of Prospero's banishment sounds like a condensation of one of the monitory accounts in the *Mirror for Magistrates* which shows that the ruler must forever vigilantly exercise himself to judge aright his counselors' honesty and reliability.

Caliban, however, is hard to place among standard dramatic conventions. Curiously, he attracts as much attention from modern speculators as he must have from Shakespeare's audience—and perhaps the same kind of wonder. So gross a figure is surely out of place in romance, altogether an intruder. Actually, he derives from creatures familiar to Elizabethan auditors and viewers of pageants, but in this dramatic milieu he seems an exotic. He has some of the function of the wild man of satirical plays and pageants, who inveighs against the world and points out the follies of the time. But Caliban's sophistication is, ironically, quite insular and his complaints limited to laments for the baseness of human nature, so like his own, evident in the rogues whom he has taken for his masters.

Over these conflicts and tensions there reigns a twofold control: the traditional natural correspondences, which metaphorically assure us of the existence of an order responsive to a higher will, and the religion of love which, again metaphorically, is the instrumental relationship whereby that higher will fashions and maintains creation's good bondage to abstract virtue—the goodness that *is* nature as well as the goodness of nature's operation.

The first manifestation of this twofold control is the storm itself, responsive to Prospero's wishes and manipulated by Ariel. Surely the storm metaphorically signifies the power (Ariel refers to it as destiny) "that hath to instrument this lower world, / And what is in it . . ." (III.iii.54–55). Nature on the island, furthermore, as well as corresponding item for item with the nature of the islanders, also controls them. Fogs, damps, and frost assail the brutal Caliban and his loutish companions; strange noises affright and warn the highborn plotters and their intended victim. The island itself is a metaphor of the cosmos watched over by a beneficent power. Note, however, how much of the standard comparison of macrocosm and microcosm Shakespeare omits. He has so concentrated the references to nature and man's correspondent being that we have, in effect, the object to which comparison is made but not the object which is being compared. That is to say, we have no kingdom of this world compared to the ideal realm of natural order. We apprehend directly the natural order and the ordering power.

The second aspect of the way in which control is exercised (over the play as well as over the special world of which it speaks) is the convention of the religion of love. The love conventions in *The Tempest*, however, are simplified so as to give us romance in its pristine form. Thus, the wooing of Miranda begins with love at first sight, the simple, direct, uncomplicated yet precise emotion. "At first sight they have changed eyes," comments Prospero, well pleased with the way destiny can use this lower world for its high purposes. Yet, lest there be too easy success, he commands obedience to the code so as to ensure in the hearts and minds of the lovers themselves the soundness of the match:

> But this swift business
> I must uneasy make, lest too light winning
> Make the prize light.
>   [I.ii.450–52]

The love game prescribes just such duties and behavior as will serve Prospero's intention. The convention which, for instance, demands that the lover prove worthy of his lady's favor is a test of the quality of his love:

> The very instant that I saw you, did
> My heart fly to your service.
> [III.i.64–65]

Thus Ferdinand. Unfortunately, the "service" involves the ignoble task, more fit for Caliban, of lugging firewood about. The significance of this humiliation is not lost upon the young prince, who realizes that his vow of fidelity is being tested. Similarly, the honesty of his love is underlined by his reactions to Prospero's stern warnings against premarital knowledge, which are not harsh, crabbed, apprehensive old age speaking,[1] but a further test of the wholesomeness of his love.

Ferdinand then, with unsurprising conformity to the old tradition, becomes a devotee in the religion of love. Thereafter, the ritual appropriate to the religion of love most fittingly enhances the play's closing scene, as the masque of Ceres makes visible for a moment the joy that reigns in heaven when love of man and woman is orderly and devout. The masque is fitting prelude to the last scene in which Prospero, like the rulers of courts of earlier plays (the court of the prince who acts the role of the lord of love in romantic comedy, and the actual king's court in history and tragedy), distributes rewards and punishments, all tempered by forgiveness to which even the bad are forced to yield, feeling their viciousness, without their willing it, subdued.

The Tempest is worthy summation of Shakespeare's skill. It is the supreme example of his art of calculated synthesis, combining elements of drama over which he had gained mastery, uniting them now in his last play in an alloy of transcendent virtue. Perhaps a better way of saying it would be to use the conventional terminology of the play itself. In the last analysis, the means by which that power (the destiny referred to by Ariel and embodied in Prospero) directs its "instrument," this lower world, is the shows and pageants, the stories, legends, and plays—all no more, and no less, substantial than the great globe itself. The conventions which shape the plays and shows are the lifeblood, the means, the structure, and the necessary order of that shaping and directing power. Never before have they been so visible, never so completely seen as in themselves they really are, as in *The Tempest,* wherein the pure conventions are acted out so that what they symbolize becomes immediately apparent—all intervening stuff between the judicious spectator and a world in which symbol *is* actuality being pushed aside. We see a world, in short, where form and content are identical. And this is, of course, the supreme achievement of art.

This study was undertaken with no prior commitment to a conclusion. In the course of tracing the principal conventions, however, there became apparent the greater use Shakespeare made of the apparatus of the natural correspondences and of the religion-of-love metaphor than of the other conventions. At first he delighted in playing fantastic tricks of dramaturgy with them, but in the end used them as the most satisfying, the most nearly perfect means of presenting his audience with a well-made play that would also be the embodiment of what his audience, and, as nearly as we can tell, he himself had always believed and were satisfied to continue believing about the nature of man and the universe. This conclusion makes of Shakespeare somewhat less than a revolutionary, and there is, to be sure, some justification for Bernard Shaw's condemning Shakespeare because Shakespeare left the world as he found it. But it makes a difference which world is meant. Shaw's was a smaller world, and, to his credit, he helped change it. Shakespeare's is a larger world, and he helped preserve it.

What, in the final analysis, is there in Shakespeare's plays that at once portrays the world and helps preserve it? How do Shakespeare's modesty and cunning cooperate in this endeavor of art? In examining Shakespeare's uses of traditional themes, characters, and narrative patterns, we have seen him incorporate them ever more cunningly into the fabric and machinery of the mature plays and the last comedies. If we dare, we can essay a formula or pattern for the archetypal Shakespearean drama. The question of how his mind worked, how he set about drafting a play, why he chose this or that course, how he adapted the source—all of these speculations seem to yield significant answers when asked in the context of Shakespeare's use of literary tradition. It seems not too bold, then, to draft a working plan that he might have evolved during his apprentice and journeyman years. In brief outline such a plan would be somewhat like this: Shakespeare chooses sources that offer a maximum opportunity for extracting in a calculated way multiple tensions of character, plot, and theme. These are arranged so as to arrive finally at a balance resulting from the pairing of these tension-producing elements in characters compounded from clichés, in familiar narrative patterns disrupted and then resumed, in received opinions ironically examined and, at the point of almost irretrievable subversion, reaffirmed. Wherever we look, we see this calculation at work (a long-continued, calculated deception that yields at last to a final clarification at the end of the play might be another way of describing Shakespeare's dramaturgy).

What I have been saying is a disclaimer to the view that Shakespeare, working under the close demands of the season at the Globe, in the very process of hasty composition merely struck out unreflectingly these happy phrases and novel combinations. Unlike Racine and Corneille, masters of elegance and sublimity, Shakespeare—many like to imagine—never really bothered about taking pains. He wrote by inspiration, responding instinctively to the pressures of getting a new play on the boards twice a year. He seized the thunderbolts as they flew by. By some such miracle he united haphazard inspiration with fine craftsmanship. There was no pacing the floor in his lodgings on the Bankside, no wrestling with problems of phrasing, scene construction, or unity of dramatic action.

Actually, there is no miracle in Shakespeare's dramaturgy save his almost unfailing knowledge of what would bind the audience to him. Miracle enough, to be sure, but not the miracle of chance inspiration. Shakespeare did indeed grapple with the problems of dramaturgy, but, employing shrewdness and calculation in exploiting conventional material, he compressed the arduous work of planning and plotting and characterization from months into weeks. The point is that Shakespeare's "cleverness" in utilizing conventional material is in a very real way the secret of his success. We have, after all, no technique sophisticated enough to account for the complexities of the process of artistic creation. But we can at least observe some of the process occurring in the particular milieu of Shakespeare's drama.

As we have noted in the first chapter, E. E. Stoll discerned in Shakespeare's plays a calculated use of contrast.[2] Stoll's books shone with brilliant insights. But he never, it seems to me, gave credit enough to a principal source of Shakespeare's greatest success—the audience. For without the audience's familiarity with an extensive body of conventions, the contrasts would not have been so dramatically effective. Nor would the playwright have repeatedly essayed so subtle an approach to drama as to try to surprise by contrasting the familiar and strange or by adding two familiar elements together so as to achieve something new and strange. Shakespeare most certainly would not have tried it repeatedly had he not learned to trust his audience. He might well have tried for the same kind of success that Jonson enjoyed with his castigation of obvious and often outmoded social types and follies or the making of topical jokes at the expense of the fools and fantastics of his time.

Nor did Stoll pay sufficient attention to the fact that Shakespeare makes something of the contrasts with which he surprises us. In his impatience with critics bent upon psychoanalyzing Hamlet, Stoll left Hamlet a creature of isolated moments of existence, a figure of one brilliant, momentary impact after another. But if we are sensitive to the traditions that have contributed to Hamlet's being, we see that some coherent, though complex, view of man evolves—a many-sided view, to be sure, but in its complexity truly an expression of the soul of the age. Stoll would hesitate, of course, to ascribe to Shakespeare the consciously held design of giving tongue and image to the soul of the age, but it seems to me quite credible that

Shakespeare in learning how to create character, narrative, and theme from the manifold literary tradition was dealing with precisely those expressions which summarized the moral, political, and religious beliefs of his time and made them his own. In short, his is the secret of great drama—how to make an idea or an abstraction live in symbol on stage.

How vexed a question this is of the interplay of morality, dramatic conventions, and the reactions of playwright, audience, and critic can be illustrated by referring once again to Northrop Frye's *A Natural Perspective*. Romantic conventions, to adapt Frye's argument, such as the honest lover and his protestations are structural parts of a romantic play and do not necessarily indicate that the author is an honest lover himself or a proselytizer for the religion of love. But the dramatist finds that if he incorporates the stereotype character of honest lover as part of the structure of his play, he must by the logic of dramatic construction (which of course requires dramatic conflict in order to operate) incorporate also the foolish lover. Then (I believe that Frye neglects this point) in giving his characters speech and motive, the playwright necessarily endows them with a moral nature. For a character on stage can no more exist without making morally significant choices and statements than can a human being in actual society. Nevertheless, some critics suspect that conventional moral statements weaken a play's structure. Frye himself, after wisely pointing out the necessity of accepting a play's dramatic conventions in order to understand the play itself, sometimes condemns characterizations based on these very conventions. Thus we find Frye scolding those who would concern themselves overmuch with the major ideas of the age as embodied in Shakespeare's plays, as if Shakespeare were spokesman for the age.[3]

One might reply to this that Shakespeare's beliefs are not necessarily indicated in his plays—granted. It is not necessary to belabor the point. Nevertheless, one cannot overlook the significance of Shakespeare's consistently dealing with the major ideas of his age, incorporating them repeatedly (as motivations for characters) into the very structure of his plays, giving them voice so as to convince again of their worth an audience already predisposed to believe. The major ideas are themselves vital parts of the characterizations; the characterizations are conventions. Hence, the ideas function as dramatic conventions. It is difficult, moreover, to see how Shakespeare and his audience can be believers inside the theater and not outside. It seems far more likely, morally and psychologically, that the same beliefs obtain inside and outside the theater, with the dramatic conventions providing the firm bond between esthetic and moral commitments.

It is, furthermore, difficult to be consistent in giving conventions their due weight throughout a discussion of Shakespeare's plays. Frye, for example, makes his most persuasive argument when discussing *Macbeth: Macbeth* is not a play about the moral crime of murder; it is a play about the dramatically conventional crime of killing the lawful and anointed king.[4] The convention gives a ritual quality to the action that enables the playwright to identify the actors with the powers of nature. The lawful king, then, has a bond with the ordering principle or power in nature. The murdering usurper is associated with the powers of chaos and darkness. Without this conventional element, the play would degenerate into a grotesque melodrama.

This is certainly a sound argument. When he deals with some other plays, however, Frye seems not to hold quite so fast to the principle of accepting the dramatic conventions as a first step in criticism. For example, in his discussion of *Cymbeline*,[5] his eagerness to call attention to the impossibilities and improbabilities of the plot betrays him into the same fault he has blamed others for, that is, pointing out ludicrous characterizations and plot deficiencies and failing to discern that the conventions which include such implausibilities are integral in the play's structure.

It appears, then, that Shakespeare uses conventional literary material in three ways in shaping his plays, employing it as a master pattern, so to speak, which guides his adaptation of sources as well as his contriving of original work. He fashions alloys from familiar character types; he employs narrative patterns that move to foregone conclusions, but which because of cunning disruptions along the way no longer seem trite; and he subjects received opinions to the test of irony and skepticism. The result is a maximum amount of irony, the audience being repeatedlyoffered the opportunity of reacting to the paradox of familiar novelty.

The conventions that make up the religion of love and the doctrine of the natural correspondences become Shakespeare's chief reliance because they so precisely answer the structural demands of a play fashioned from traditional material yet viable as a many-dimensioned drama. For he was (a point that cannot be insisted upon too much) a very practical dramatist. The conventions are, moreover, doubly valuable in incorporating the edification his audience expected into the structure of the play. The religion of love has built-in stock characterizations, for example, as well as a metaphorical content that relates most satisfactorily both to social codes and to religious assumptions. Similarly, the natural correspondences provide a series of references for establishing theme and creating character. The correspondences convey, moreover, a metaphorical intimation of an assured order, moral as well as natural, without which a playwright is hard put to it to write tragedy—witness the frustrations present-day dramatists experience. These standard sets of conventional metaphors and stock characters, then, all manipulated by Shakespeare in his unique way, greatly enable him to impose order on the chaos of existence and, in terms of the play and audience response to it, employ motives and moral significances as structural elements.

This unification of dramatic structure and ethical significance is, perhaps, the chief reason for Shakespeare's being so remarkably the mentor of Western culture. A survey of Shakespeare as modest and cunning manipulator of familiar conventions and calculator of audience reactions can go at least part of the way to aid in understanding the appeal of his drama to the Globe audience. We need, however, to add that these apparently outmoded conventions are, even today, the heart and fiber of his plays, his altars still green with ancient bays. From such conventions is constructed what is to our aesthetic sense an orderly, meaningful exposition of life.

Notes

CHAPTER ONE

1. In *Perspectives of Criticism* (Cambridge, Mass., 1950).
2. Edgar E. Stoll, *Art and Artifice in Shakespeare* (New York, 1933; reprint ed., London, 1963), p. 90.
3. Donald Stauffer, *Shakespeare's World of Images* (New York, 1949), p. 75.
4. Hereward Price, "Shakespeare as Critic," *Philological Quarterly*, XX (1941), 390–99.

CHAPTER TWO

1. Both Madeleine Doran, *Endeavors of Art* (Madison, 1954), pp. 102 ff., and Muriel Bradbrook, *Growth and Structure of Elizabethan Comedy* (London, 1955), pp. 132 ff., describe this change.
2. *Art and Artifice*, p. 25.
3. *Art and Artifice*, p. 85.
4. *Art and Artifice*, p. 88.

CHAPTER THREE

1. Alfred Harbage, *Shakespeare's Audience* (New York, 1941), pp. 174–78, gives the attendance records deducible from Henslowe.
2. See, for example, H. S. Bennett, *Shakespeare's Audience, Proceedings of the British Academy* (London, 1944).
3. Here I follow Alfred Harbage (*Shakespeare's Audience*, 1941) whose carefully documented conclusions seem to me altogether sound.

4. Edward Arber, *Transcript of the Registers of the Company of Stationers*, 5 vols. (London, 1875–94), II, 23.

5. Holinshed's *Chronicles* were first published in two folio volumes, 1577. A second edition in three volumes appeared in 1587. Hakluyt's *Voyages* appeared in 1589; 3 volumes 1598–1600; one volume 1599. Stow's *Survey* saw many editions and additions: 1598, 1603, 1618; continued and enlarged 1633. The many editions of his *Chronicles, Survey* and *Annals* take up a column and a half of the *Short Title Catalogue.*

6. Erasmus, *De Conscribendis Epistolis* (Antwerp, 1566). Both an intending wooer and a writer of romantic comedy could benefit from Erasmus's digest of themes and conventions of the lover's code which he sets forth (p. 263) as a guide for writing letters: "Quod si puellas animum ad mutuum amorem sollicitabimus, duobus potissimum arietibus utemur, laude & misericordia. . . . Summum amorem, cum summa desperatione conjunctum ostendemus . . . exemplis utemur illustrium & honestarum mulierum, quae honestissimum conabimur ostendere."

7. E. K. Chambers, *Elizabethan Stage*, 4 vols. (Oxford, 1951), IV, 159.

8. L. C. Knights, "Education and the Drama in the Age of Shakespeare," *Criterion*, XI (1931–32), 607: ". . . of any typical audience at, say, the Globe the majority were likely to have received an education of the grammar school type." See also T. W. Baldwin, *Shakespeare's Small Latine and Lesse Greeke*, 2 vols. (Urbana, 1956). In the second volume Baldwin examines the curricula of both the lower and upper grammar schools of the sixteenth century. A. L. Rowse, *The England of Elizabeth* (New York, 1961), pp. 489–533, also surveys the history and curricula of the many schools founded during Elizabeth's reign.

9. L. B. Wright, *Middle Class Culture in Elizabethan England* (Chapel Hill, 1935), pp. 52–62, quotes from the guild and school records.

10. The condemnatory phrase is from William London, *A Catalogue of the most vendible Books in England*, 1657. Quoted by Wright, *Middle Class Culture*, p. 86.

11. Their titles indicate their biases: Stephen Gosson, *Playes Confuted in five Actions, Proving that they are not to be suffered in a Christian commonweale* (1582), and *The School of Abuse, Containing a pleasaunt invective against Poets, Pipers, Plaiers,*

Jesters and such like Caterpillars of the Commonwealth (1579, 1587); Philip Stubbes, *The Anatomy of Abuses* (1583; 4th ed. 1595).

12. London *Observer*, May 29, 1960, p. 9.

CHAPTER FOUR

1. Chambers, *Elizabethan Stage*, vol. I, chap. 10, and T. W. Baldwin, *Organization and Personnel of the Shakespearean Company* (Princeton, 1927), pp. 10 ff.
2. The dates assigned to Shakespeare's plays are, for the most part, those given by Chambers, *Elizabethan Stage*, III, 481–89. Lines quoted from the plays are numbered according to Kittredge's *Complete Works of Shakespeare* (New York, 1936).
3. Alfred Harbage, *As They Liked It* (New York, 1961), p. 13.
4. Doran, *Endeavors of Art*, p. 325.
5. *Endeavors of Art*, p. 347.
6. Northrop Frye, *A Natural Perspective* (New York, 1965), p. 12.
7. Stauffer, *Shakespeare's World of Images*, p. 75.
8. *A Natural Perspective*, p. 81.
9. J. C. Collins, *Plays and Poems of Robert Greene*, 2 vols. (Oxford, 1905), I, 57.
10. Reprinted, London, 1837, p. 259.
11. "Translating Shakespeare," *Literary Moscow*, 1956. Translated by Manya Harari and reprinted in *I Remember: Sketch for an Autobiography* (New York, 1959), p. 140.
12. Although Bernard Spivack, *Shakespeare and the Allegory of Evil* (New York, 1958), does not mention Gobbo as an example, he describes the combinations in sixteenth-century drama of the intriguer with a figure of fun and mockery. Gobbo might well serve as a minor example of this sort of combination.
13. J. W. Cunliffe, *Early English Tragedies* (Oxford, 1912), p. lxxv.
14. Chambers, *Elizabethan Stage*, III, 22.
15. See especially Bernard Spivack, *Shakespeare and the Allegory of Evil*, p. 204, who discusses the hybrid quality of Falstaff's character. Falstaff embodies all of the menace of the serious Vice of the morality, but his jests make it difficult for the modern audience to regard him as a villain in any sense.
16. Evadne has caused trouble for a great many critics. Fredson Bowers, *Elizabethan Revenge Tragedy* (Princeton, 1940), p. 174, for example, says that such a scene as her changing from

scornful adulteress to eager revenger of injury was a favorite with Beaumont and Fletcher and excited "the admiration of their audience." Earlier, however (p. 134 n.), Bowers notes that Fletcher "titillates a jaded audience with strong situations." One might conclude that a jaded audience and a vitiated drama were the results of these techniques of shock and surprise used as dramatic ends in themselves.

17. *Horizon*, September, 1960, p. 53.

CHAPTER FIVE

1. *New York Times*, February 19, 1950.
2. *An Apology for Actors*, 1612, F$_3$verso–F$_4$recto.
3. For example, T. M. Parrott, *Shakespeare: Twenty-Three Plays* (New York, 1953), p. 633. "Shakespeare wrote *Julius Caesar* not to teach any political lesson, but to exhibit on the stage a great action and to give immortal life to the actors in that deed."
4. Harbage, *As They Liked It*, p. 104.
5. Chambers, *Elizabethan Stage*, III, 431–32.
6. Pp. 40 ff.
7. Here I follow O. J. Campbell, *Shakespeare's Satire* (Oxford, 1943), pp. 99–100, who cites approvingly Peter Alexander's conclusion (*The Library*, 4th series, IX, 277–78) that *Troilus and Cressida* was composed for an Inns of Court audience.

CHAPTER SIX

1. See, for example, Clifford Leech's discovery of harshness of tone in *The Tempest. Shakespeare's Tragedies* (New York, 1950), pp. 137–58.
2. See note 2, chap. 1, above.
3. *A Natural Perspective*, pp. 40 ff.
4. *A Natural Perspective*, p. 62.
5. *A Natural Perspective*, p. 68.

Index

173